D0759616

Cybernetic
Engineering

Cybernetic
Engineering

JOHN F. YOUNG
BSc CGIA MIEE MIERE

A HALSTED PRESS BOOK

JOHN WILEY & SONS
New York–Toronto

Published in the U.S.A. and Canada
by Halsted Press, a Division
of John Wiley & Sons, Inc., New York

Library of Congress Cataloging in Publication Data

Young, John Frederick.
    Cybernetic engineering.
    "A Halsted Press book."
    Includes bibliographies.
    1. Cybernetics. I. Title.
Q310.Y65   001.53   72-7438
ISBN 0-470-97942-9

First published 1973

Printed in Hungary

Preface

For years we have used automatic devices which could carry out most complex activities, with human intervention limited perhaps to the issuing of orders. The automatic telephone exchange is a prime example. What is there to be in the future which is different? The answer is that it is now at last feasible to produce a really general purpose robot. All previous automatic devices have been designed to carry out only one or perhaps a few special operations. However, consider the situation if the general purpose robot first appears as a mass-produced domestic appliance, capable of carrying out a variety of tasks in response to orders, either from a human or from another machine. A variety of tasks, moreover, which has actually been learned by the robot in the course of its tuition.

This is no longer science fiction. We can have this situation as soon as we are prepared to spend the money on research and development. The basic robot brain, the eyes, ears and touch sensors, the fingers and the mobility have all been investigated and shown to be feasible in the course of research at Aston and elsewhere. It is only necessary to bring them all together. A tiny fraction of the money spent on space research would make the domestic robot a reality.

Inevitably, some country will spend the money. In the Cybernetics Laboratory at Aston University, the writer and his students are investigating many of the engineering aspects of the Robot. The present book deals with the work which has been carried out at Aston and elsewhere on the brain and central nervous system of the robot, both in theory and in practice.

JOHN F. YOUNG

Contents

Contents

1 | Cybernetic Engineering

1.1 CYBERBNETICS

Cybernetics[1] was defined by the late Norbert Wiener as 'The Science of Communication and Control in Animals and Machines'.[2] At first sight, this is an excellent scientific definition. Wiener certainly seemed to know just what he meant by it, and so did most of the people who worked in this field in the early nineteen-fifties.

As time went on however, more and more people became attracted to the subject. It was found that in practice the definition can be made to cover such a wide field that very little scientific activity can be excluded from the umbrella of cybernetics at all.

As an example, is Art a part of Cybernetics? The artist produces works with the intention of communicating his ideas to other human beings. Human beings are part of the animal kingdom. It follows, so the argument goes, that Art is part of Cybernetics. And so, at international conferences on cybernetics, one can find artists giving lectures on their work, particularly if the work happens to have been produced on a machine tool controlled by numerically punched tape. One recent art exhibition was in fact called the 'Cybernetic Serendipity' exhibition. Very similar arguments have been used for the introduction of architecture under the blanket cover of cybernetics.

If the definition adopted by Wiener is to be accepted, then there seems to be no reason why cybernetics should not bring together many different arts and scientific disciplines. Some people would even go further than this. For example, it has been seriously suggested at a conference on cybernetics[5] that some chemical reactions are cybernetic in nature because they involve what might be called a feedback process. And the argument goes that anything which involves some form of feedback must be part of cybernetics. It is, according to such arguments, not even necessary that a feedback loop be involved.

The resulting situation is somewhat confused. This would not be too bad if the world was not at present suffering from an 'information explosion'. It is extremely time consuming to wade through masses

1

of published information in the hope of finding one paper which might be of some importance.

The discipline of cybernetics can be said to have started with the work and thoughts of Descartes on the methods of operation and control of the human body. One is impressed when one reads some of the works of Descartes and his contemporaries by the range of knowledge which they had and by the very modernity of their thoughts. Some of the guesses which were made at that time about the bodily mechanism were of course quite incorrect, and it was some two centuries later before the modern concept of homeostasis could be introduced into the study of the nervous system.

The human and animal nervous systems act as regulator systems which maintain, for example, the temperature of the body within close limits. In the mid-1940's, it began to be appreciated that such actions are very similar to those of engineering control systems, for example of thermostats in temperature control systems. It was then that Wiener coined the convenient name of 'Cybernetics'.

There had been, even prior to this time, attempts to make useful robots, and devices such as artificial photoelectrically guided 'tortoises' had been produced since early in this century. The attraction of the 'Metal Man' form of humanoid robot was obvious, and various forms had been exhibited. The introduction of various forms of guided missile into warfare made it clear that mobile robot devices could certainly be produced.

However, the limitations of the early devices were obvious. The range of activities which they could undertake depended on the complexity of the central control mechanism, and if this had to be carried around by the robot, then the size and versatility was limited. The introduction of the digital computer brought the promise of a greater complexity of control, but unfortunately early digital computers were enormous in size and cost. Now that modern circuitry techniques are making possible a considerable reduction in the size of electronic computers, the use of such devices for the control of mobile robots is becoming more practicable. At the same time, cybernetic engineering investigations such as those described in the present book are introducing techniques which promise even further reduction of the size and weight of the 'brain' of the mobile robot.

1.2 CYBERNETIC SYSTEMS

In essence, cybernetics deals with some types of system. The sort of system which can be considered in cybernetics is well-illustrated by the analogy drawn by the late Warren McCulloch.[7] McCulloch considered the flow of information in the nervous system of an animal or of a human. He compared this flow with the flow of water in a river.

The tributary streams converge and combine in the mainstream of the river. Then, at the sea, the water in the river again diverges in the delta at the mouth of the river. The process is called Anastomosis.

McCulloch compared this action with the way in which, in the nervous system of an animal or of a human, electrical impulses flow from the peripheral nerve endings, along the afferent nerve fibres to converge on the central nervous system formed by the spinal column and by the brain. In the central nervous system of the animal, the information about the environmental conditions of the body is mixed, just as the waters are mixed in the main stream of a river. From the central nervous system, the efferent nerve fibres carry away impulses to control the muscles of the body.

McCulloch's analogy gives an attractive way of considering the action of the animal nervous system in isolation. However, the nervous system is never actually in isolation; it always performs in an active environment, an environment upon which the nervous system acts and which in turn reacts upon the nervous system.

In the writer's cybernetics laboratory, the analogy given by McCulloch has been extended in order to take into account this vital interaction between the environment and the nervous system. The delta of the river discharges water into the surrounding sea. From there, the water evaporates. Some of the water vapour is blown back over the land, and there is precipitation of rain, hail or snow. The precipitation falls upon the land, from where some of it finds its way back into the tributary streams of the river.

The whole system forms a loop. Now it is very important to note that this is not an entirely closed loop as in the classical man-made control system. It is instead a loop which is capable of interaction with other similar loops and also with the environment in general. Cybernetics can be said to be the study of such loops. It is closely related to the field of Control Systems, in which the loops studied are, in the main, non-interacting.

The relatively new discipline of Information Theory[8] has appeared and grown almost concurrently with that of Cybernetics, and there appears to have been some tendency to group the two together. However, information theory deals only with the theory and efficiency of communication of information from one individual or machine to another. The important control aspects of cybernetics are completely missing from information theory studies.

Consequently the latter can be regarded as a subdivision of the former. However, the direct application of information theory in the field of cybernetics is most limited, and the grouping does not seem useful.

1.3 CYBERNETIC ENGINEERING

It is an unfortunate fact that the definition of cybernetics is so wide that the term has been degraded. The process has continued to the point where the use of the term to describe any one particular aspect of work has the effect of conveying no information. As time goes on, more and more people from different fields lay claim to be working in the field of cybernetics so that there is a real need for some form of sub-division of the subject.

The sub-division in which the writer works mainly, and which is the subject of this book, can be called Cybernetic Engineering. This field can be defined as the application to engineering of devices and techniques derived from biology.

The process of cybernetic engineering is by no means new. In the past, the engineer has always studied biological mechanisms in order to obtain ideas for application to some of his new engineering devices. In recent years the application of this approach has accelerated and has been more deliberate.

Perhaps it should be emphasised that in cybernetic engineering there is not normally any attempt to produce a perfect and rigidly detailed copy or model of any biological mechanism. Instead, the intention is to adopt only the overall mode of operation of a biological mechanism in order to achieve an engineering aim. At our present state of knowledge, direct copying is in any case an impossibility, since we do not yet know how to make even the basic building blocks or cells from which the biological mechanisms are constructed. A simple example will make clear the methods adopted in cybernetic engineering.

For centuries, man observed the ease with which birds and insects achieved flight, though he attempted in vain to copy their methods. It was only when man finally abandoned his attempts to produce a direct copy of the animal methods of flight that success was finally achieved. While the overall mode of gliding flight was retained, all else was dropped. It is perhaps unnecessary to point out that if this method of progress had not been adopted, then we would not, even today, have achieved heavier-than-air flight. There are as yet no successful man-carrying flapping-wing aircraft.

In cybernetic engineering, as will be seen in this book, the same process is being deliberately adopted in order to achieve the eventual aim, the construction of useful and reliable, yet economical, humanoid robots and robot devices. Study of, for example, the eye of an insect can suggest to the engineer ways in which he might construct a device performing a similar function. Because of this, the cybernetic engineer must carry out extensive studies of biological systems and in particular, biological nervous systems.

1.4 BIONICS

As if there was not enough confusion existing in the field of cybernetics, a further difficulty has been produced by the introduction of the word Bionics, by the United States Air Force.[9] Bionics has been defined as the art of applying knowledge of biological systems and methods to the solution of engineering problems. However, the originator of this term has given a different definition: 'The science of systems whose function is based on living systems, or which have the characteristics of living systems, or which resemble these'.

It has been suggested that in bionics, physical systems are studied and realised by analogy with living systems, while in cybernetics, living systems are studied by analogy with physical systems. However, there are not many who would accept such a restriction of the field of cybernetics.

Now it seems that bionics is very similar to cybernetic engineering, so why should not the former term be adopted in preference? There is a very clear reason, and it lies in the confusion caused by the very form of the name bionics. One would surely be justified in assuming that the word bionics is formed from a combination of the words biology and electronics. However, it seems that this obvious explanation is simply not the true one.

We are told that the word was apparently built up from the Greek word *bion*, meaning 'unit of life'. It seems most undesirable that such confusion should be possible in the basic word used to describe any branch of science. Would it not be better to drop such a word quietly from an already overcrowded scientific vocabulary? This would have the additional advantage of removing any possibility of confusion between cybernetic engineering and the 'Bion', introduced by Wilhelm Reich.

1.5 ROBOTICS

One aim of cybernetics is the investigation, design and construction of Robots of various types. In the past, unfortunately, the field of Robotics has tended to be associated with fiction. Now, however, technology has advanced to the point where the useful mobile robot is an immediate possibility. Already, remotely-controlled mobile robot devices have been used under dangerous conditions, for example in conditions of radioactivity. Non-mobile robots, capable of learning to perform an industrial task and then of being left to perform it tirelessly, are even now in use in industrial plants all over the world, and their use is spreading.

At the present time there is a considerable body of knowledge of Robotics, and this has been documented by the writer in the companion book 'Robotics'. Robotics can be taken to deal with the physical action of the robot, with the relationship between the robot and the external world. Thus Robotics deals with the arms and hands, with the motive methods, with the sense organs, the eyes and ears of the useful robot, as well as with such important factors as reliability. Cybernetic engineering, on the other hand, deals with the 'brain' and the 'nervous system' of the useful, learning, robot. It is concerned with the control of the mechanism of the robot.

Those mobile robots which have been constructed in the past are generally one of three types.

The first type is intended merely for entertainment or as a child's toy, and will not be further dealt with here. The second type is in effect an extension of a human operator, and the term 'Telechiric' device, from the Greek for 'distant hand', has sometimes been applied to this type.

The third type of robot is capable of carrying out a task when ordered to by a human, in independence of direct and detailed command. It is this type of robot with which we are chiefly concerned in cybernetic engineering. In general, such robots have been controlled up to the present time by large digital computers, and in consequence the overall cost is prohibitive. Nevertheless, the results obtained have been most impressive. The Japanese Hitachi 'Hivip', for example, can read an engineering drawing with one television eye, and find the necessary parts and assemble them to the drawing using another television eye and a mechanical hand and arm. A large computer is needed for control at present, and the action is very slow, each decision requiring a great deal of computation.

Nevertheless, the success of such independent robots is most impressive. It is hoped that cybernetic engineering will be able to reduce the cost and to increase the speed of action of the robot to the point where it becomes practicable to use it not only in production on the factory shop-floor, but also domestically. When the successful domestic robot appears, the resulting economy of scale will bring the price down to the point where it will be widely used in industry as well as in the home.

1.6 CONDITIONAL PROBABILITY

A certain amount of work has been carried out, mainly in theory only, on the use of conditional probability.[10, 11] Conditional probability will be discussed in more detail later. It is sufficient to point out at this stage that the use of conditional probability in cybernetic systems necessitates the addition of special extra facilities for the forget-ting process. This necessity is overcome completely if joint probabilities are used, rather than conditional probabilities, in a memory system.[14]

This is despite suggestions which have been made to the contrary, and which seem to have guided quite an amount of theoretical work. However, such work does not appear to have received practical veri-fication and will be criticised in more detail at a later stage.

For the present, suffice it to note that if there is a certain number, say n, of nerve cells in an organism, then it has been said that the nerv-ous system of the organism must be capable of recognising a total of 2^n different patterns. In order to do this, it has been argued, it is necessary to have arrangements in any nervous system which are capable of discriminating between these different patterns.

That such a point of view is nonsensical can be very easily demon-strated. Consider the human brain. It is known to have of the order of 10^{10}, or ten thousand million, different nerve cells. Now in order to obtain an over-estimate, let us suppose that each one of these nerve cells in the brain is capable of discriminating a completely different pattern of activity of the total number n of nerve cells in the body which can provide inputs to the brain. In order to simplify the prob-lem, suppose further that each of the input nerve cells is only capable of a binary form of activity, that is that it is either on or it is off.

Now the n nerve cells in the body can then produce a total of 2^n different patterns of activity. Each of the total of 10^{10} cells in the brain is supposed to respond to one only of these patterns of activity. The question can now be asked: 'What is the maximum number n of human nerve cells which the human brain is capable of handling?'

The answer is obtained by simply solving the equation: $2^n = 10^{10}$. If we take logarithms to base 10, we obtain:

$$n \log 2 = 10$$

and therefore:

$$n = \frac{10}{\log 2} = \frac{10}{0 \cdot 301} = 33 \cdot 2$$

Now consider the full implications of the above derivation. It shows that under the simplified conditions usually accepted, the human brain would only be capable of handling the information from some 33 of the thousands of nerve cells in the human body. This is obvious nonsense. Nevertheless, the arguments that any electronic learning device ought to be capable of handling 2^n different patterns of activity are still heard,[12] and in some cases they have been used to close down important research which did not meet such an impracticable require-ment.

It will be shown later that such fallacious reasoning has been a result of over-theoretical thought, taking no regard of the actual performance of organisms. Suffice it to point out now that the mistake which has been made lies mainly in the over-concentration on patterns of inputs, and the virtual dismissal of the fact that the number of output muscles which an organism has at its disposal is vastly fewer than is the number of input nerve cells.

In this connection, it has been pointed out by Fisher of Aston that while there are about 10^8 inputs to the human brain, there are only about 200 to 300 muscular outputs to be controlled. It is probably more than coincidence that the product of these two numbers is of the order of the number of brain cells. In accordance with such information, the approach adopted in the ASTRA[13] associating machines at Aston has been:

$$\text{Inputs} \times \text{Outputs} = \text{Store Locations.}$$

However, in order to achieve satisfactory performance despite such a reduction in store size, it appears to be essential to add the feature of inhibition to a learning device, whether animal or machine.

REFERENCES

1. YOUNG, J. F., *Cybernetics*, Iliffe/Elsevier (1969)
2. WIENER, N., *Cybernetics*, Wiley (1948)
3. YOUNG, J. F., What Is Cybernetics, *Nature*, **226**, 774, May 23 (1970)
4. YOUNG, J. F., 'Machine Intelligence' *Nature*, **230**, 260, March 26 (1971)
5. ROSE, J., (ed), *Progress of Cybernetics*, Gordon and Breach (1970)
6. ROSE, J., (ed) *Survey of Cybernetics*, Iliffe (1970)
7. MCCULLOCH, W. S., Spoken Statement in Film *The Living Machine*, National Film Board of Canada (1961)
8. YOUNG, J. F., *Information Theory*, Butterworth (1970)
9. LINDGREN, N., 'Bionics', *Electronics*, **135**, 37, Feb. 9 (1962)
10. UTTLEY, A. M., 'The Design of Conditional Probability Computers', *Information and Control*, **2**, 1 (1959)
11. UTTLEY, A. M., 'Properties of Plastic Networks', *Biophysics J.*, **2**, 169 (1962)
12. UTTLEY, A. M., 'Models of Memory', *New Scientist* **46**, 634 (1970)
13. YOUNG, J. F. and NRDC, British Patent Application No. 30657/68
14. YOUNG, J. F., 'Possibilities of a Sinusoidal Memory for an Extendable Cybernetic Machine', *JIERE*, **39**, 9 (1970)

2 | Background Work

2.1 THE HOMEOSTAT

An early machine which received very wide publicity was known as the Homeostat.[1] This comprised four meter movements, each having four operating coils. One of the operating coils was driven from a local electronic amplifier, while the other three were driven from the electronic ampflifiers associated with the other three electric meter movements.

Also operated by each electronic amplifier was a uniselector which switched various values of resistance into attenuators connected with the other amplifiers, so in effect changing the gain from one amplifier to the next. The meter coils moved a meter needle which dipped into a bath of electrolyte, which acted as a variable potentiometer at the input to the amplifier.

Any change from a stable condition, with all four meter needles at the central position, is followed by operation of the four uniselectors in a slow and often prolonged search for a stable condition. As each uniselector moves, it changes the attenuation in the other three circuits and so on.

The machine does nothing but search for a stable position whenever it is disturbed. The search is made at random, and there is no learning action whatsoever. The writer has suggested elsewhere[3] that the machine can be compared with the mythical room-full of monkeys, all hitting typewriter keys at random, who might, one day, write the plays of Shakespeare. The homeostat is in effect a 'floundering-machine', and it is quite useless. However, this has not prevented the publication of an extensive body of theory based on the homeostat.[2]

2.2 MISCELLANEOUS CYBERNETIC WORK

There are several studies which are regarded as coming within the scope of cybernetics, and yet which cannot be regarded as a primary part of cybernetic engineering or of great immediate interest to the cybernetic engineer. For example, the field of finite automata seems to be almost as purely mathematical now as when it was originated.

The construction of game-playing machines and the programming of computers to play games such as chess might some day lead to results which are of use to the cybernetic engineer. However, the artificial nature of the problems which are dealt with makes such work of little practical use at the present time.

Teaching machines of many different forms have been made and sold commercially. While such work can certainly be regarded as engineering, it is a very specialised and commercial field and it will not be further considered here. It is an unfortunate fact that the rival theories upon which the designs of teaching machines are based add some confusion to the subject of cybernetics, and it is hoped that the controversies may be resolved without too much delay.

Another aspect of cybernetics which will not be considered in the present book is that of automatic language translation. This subject is of great potential interest to the cybernetic engineer. However, the problems involved are at present largely those of the analysis of the structure of language rather than those of engineering construction and simulation.

2.3 ENGINEERING POSSIBILITIES OF FINITE AUTOMATA

There has been much work on the mathematics of finite automata, but very little of this has led to any practical engineering application. There has, however, been some very limited attempt to find a viable engineering application.

In a second order Markov chain[4] the probability of occurrence of each event depends on the nature of the previous event. In such a system, it is possible, by making use of the past experience, to predict the next event in a sequence in the form of a probability of occurrence.

If, in such a system, a wrong prediction is made of the next event, the incorrect nature of the prediction can be regarded as having a certain importance or significance. For conciseness, this is called the error cost, and it is possible to construct an error-cost matrix showing the relative importance of the various possible correct and incorrect predictions of the next event when any particular event is known to have just occurred.

If a machine is used to perform the prediction, then the error-cost matrix can be regarded as expressing the aptitude of the machine at performing its prediction task, since the smaller the error-cost the better is the prediction of the machine.

Such a machine must evolve or change as the external events proceed and the probabilities consequently change. The machine can change in various ways. For example, the state at which the machine starts can change, the number of different states which the machine can take, the transitions of the machine or the actual predictions made can all change. This is sometimes regarded as mutation of the machine though the biological implications of the word mutation in connection with evolution of species makes it a very undesirable term to use in this context.

It has been suggested that random changes should be made in the error matrix and these should then be evaluated and compared on the basis of error cost and that these changes which take place should proceed continuously until a decision or prediction is required.

An attempt has been made to use this sort of technique to model and to predict the output temperature of a cooling tower.[5] The results of such experiments appear to be inconclusive, and it would be most interesting to see curves of the error in prediction, rather than just the curves of the actual data and curves of the predicted data. These two separately are very difficult to interpret in published papers, and published results are disappointing.

2.4 THE MATRIX APPROACH

Any nervous system can be thought of as the embodiment of a form of matrix of nervous connections. Each row of such a matrix can be thought of as representing the input from one particular nerve sensor, while each column can be thought of as representing an output to a muscle. Reflex activity is then represented by any permanent connections built-in to the matrix. Learned activity is represented by any newly built-in connections in the matrix, formed whenever there is coincidence between a muscle output and any nerve inputs which are present, but which are not reflex to the muscle in question.

It might be argued that such a way of thinking ignored the phenomenon of inhibition, but this objection is easily overcome if some of the outputs are thought of as inhibitory outputs which prevent the operation of particular muscles (while perhaps at the same time exciting the operation of different muscles).

In basic form it is very easy to produce fixed matrices of this nature electronically, for example by the use of diode matrices. However, such a fixed matrix would not display any of the learning characteristics of the animal nervous system. In order to display learning, the cross-connections of the matrix would have to be adjustable depending on the experience of past occurrences.

This is not a difficult procedure if modern electronic techniques are utilised.

2.5 THE LERNMATRIX

A well known practical learning device which makes use of the matrix approach is the Lernmatrix due to Steinbuch, who used an array of retentive magnetic cores, like those used in computer memories, for the storage medium.[6]

It is perhaps of interest here to list some of the criteria upon which Steinbuch based the choice of magnetic cores as a storage medium.

(1) The input and the output must be in parallel (as opposed to serial) form

(2) No external supply must be required to maintain the information stored

(3) Newly learned information must not affect the stored information

(4) Read-out of the stored information must be non-destructive of the stored information

2.6 ADJUSTABLE WEIGHT MAJORITY LOGIC

In recent years there has been extensive investigation in many parts of the world into numerous forms of trainable learning machine. A variety of names,[3] such as Perceptron, Adaline and UCLM, have been applied by their makers to such devices, even though they all have almost identical principles of operation. Often the reported work has been published in such a form that, while it looks very clever, it is of no use at all to other investigators.

When examined closely, much of this work is seen to belong to a single class, which might be called the 'Adjustable-Weight, Majority Logic' approach. Much of the work which has been reported in this field relies on a deliberate reinforcing process by a human teacher, who adjusts the machine in accordance with its responses.

In this approach, each of a number of sensors, such as photo-electric cells, provides an input which is taken, via an adjustable 'weighting' resistor individual to that input, to a single common point. This common point is connected to the input terminal of an amplifier.

A given fixed procedure or strategy is then followed in order to adjust the weighting resistors in such a way as to ensure that the amplifier gives a particular value or polarity of output only when a particular given set of inputs is applied. In this way, the machine is gradually adjusted (or 'trained') to recognise patterns. The training process is carried out in general by a human operator. Convergence to a final trained state has been obtained by following certain training strategies, proved theoretically to lead to this convergence in a finite number of steps. However it is necessary to know at least one solution to the recognition problem before it is possible to estimate the length of the necessary training sequence. This fact, at the very least, has had the effect of severely limiting the value of such theoretical studies.

In such systems, there is a definite training period, followed by the achievment of a trained state. The writer has pointed out elsewhere that such systems are not well adapted to operation under changing conditions once the defined training period is over. Such a machine can only perform correctly in a fixed environment, unless it is retrained whenever the environment is seen by the operator to change.

In animal systems there is no definable training period followed by the achievment of a fully trained state. Such a system would fail to adapt to changing conditions and such failure could possibly be fatal to the organism. A single severe error of control is sufficient to produce fatality. Consequently, if such a non-adaptive process ever did occur in an organism, it would tend to be eliminated by the process of natural selection.

This fact alone would seem to explain why the animal learning process never produces complete freedom from error. Although the probability of error is reduced with the length of the training period, the necessary facility for adaptation itself ensures that error is never completely absent.

If learning machines are to have a facility for adaptation, then it would appear to be desirable that the training phase never ends, that the machines operate on a probabilistic basis, and that therefore the operation will never be completely error-free even under fixed-input conditions.

'To err is human': this appears to be a basic principle of biological control systems. There are many human examples of illusions caused by such effects.

2.7 FEEDBACK

It is sometimes stated or suggested that feedback is not a necessary feature of a learning process.[7] However, without any form of feedback, changes of environment will introduce ambiguity into the actions of a machine. The ambiguity can be made less important by the introduction of a forgetting process, but inevitably the machine can not then be completely error-free. Entirely random inputs to a non feedback machine are meaningless and cannot be used in the learning process, since in time every input would be associated with every other input.

Feedback need not, however, be deliberately built into a machine necessarily. Feedback can occur via the environment, as happens in the process of Anastomosis in the animal system as was discussed earlier. Some combinations of inputs $I(1 \ldots n)$ are associated with achievment of desirable (or positive) other inputs which are produced as a result of the actions of the outputs caused by $I(1 \ldots n)$. These will encourage continuation of that output.

Other combinations of inputs $I(p \ldots q)$ are associated with other inhibiting or negative inputs (undesirable inputs) caused by the corresponding outputs produced by $I(p \ldots q)$. These will tend to stop the output.

Consequently, feedback allows association of a particular combination of inputs with other desirable or undesirable inputs and so permits learned excitation or learned inhibition.

One very important point must not be overlooked when the feedback of information in the learning process is considered. This is that in the animal and in the human, complex tasks take some time to learn, and there are frequent errors in the course of the learning process. The human child takes a long time learning to read or to write and the adult takes some time before he can learn to coordinate new skills such as that of driving a car.

We must not expect the learning robot greatly to improve on the human in respect of this speed of learning, and it must be accepted that robot learning will be a slow process, calling for the development of specialist teaching skills. The eventual aim, of course, will be that one robot will learn from another, so relieving the human of the task of robot teaching.

2.8 USE OF DECISION THEORY AND FILTER THEORY

If any information is to be conveyed by a system of communication it follows that at the receiver there must be only a limited *a priori* knowledge of and absolutely no control over the transmitted input signal. The judgment required at the receiver involves statistical decisions.

Some of the published theoretical work on character recognition has been based on the use of statistical decision functions.[8] It is important to note that much of this work has been concerned only with the process of recognition, rather than with the process of learning to recognise. A critical part is played in the formulation and application of decision theory by *a priori* probabilities. When such probabilities do not exist, then such a theory is inapplicable.

It has been recognised that the *a priori* probabilities are unknown to the designer of a system. However instead of simply accepting the inapplicability of decision theory in such a case, it has been usual to place restrictions on the systems considered in order to make them fit the theory. In addition, the optimum theoretical decision functions have been too difficult to implement and degraded forms have been used.[9] The 'linear decision function' elements have been in effect majority logic elements as described elsewhere.

Some of the theoretical work which has been published uses a multi-dimensional representation of the input conditions. With this approach it is assumed that it is necessary to consider every possible combination of all inputs, present or absent. The receptor output for a particular input pattern is a set of numbers defining the coordinates of a vector-tip in an N-dimensional measurement space. Each vector is in effect an association between *all* inputs, whether present or absent. For example:

Inputs	A	B	C	D	E	F	G	H	Outputs
	0	0	1	0	1	0	0	1	X
	0	0	1	1	0	0	0	1	Y

The adoption of this form of representation in a practical device would necessitate the use of a great deal of equipment if more than a few inputs are to be dealt with. There are 2^N different states of N inputs. Not only would an astronomical amount of storage space be required for practical use of such a full set of vectors, but much of the space would be wasted since many of the particular combinations of inputs would be extremely unlikely to occur.

Caution is required when considering much of the published work on character recognition. Partly this is because most of it has considered not machines which learn, but only machines which can be set up manually to differentiate between characters.[10] It is stated by many writers on the subject[11] that pattern recognition machines have to be 'taught'. It is important to take great care with the use of language in this subject, and it is therefore desirable to reword this sentence by using the words 'set-up' to replace 'taught'. This removes any implications of cooperative activity on the part of the machine. The present work is directed at the design of machines which do not have to be set up, but which can inherently learn to associate certain events with certain other events which occur in the environment of the machine.

Another point is worthy of mention. Devices based on the application of decision theory will have a response which is exactly correct most of the time, but whenever an error is made at all it will be a large error. Such a response would probably be fatal in a living organism. There would be no learning about the effects of slow changes in the environment. More important, because of the occasional large errors, natural selection could be expected to operate decisively against this form of response.

Devices based on the application of filter theory,[12] are intended to minimise the mean square difference between the actual response and the desired response. Such devices are intended to discriminate continuously against large errors, though at the expense of continual small errors. Such a form of response is ideal for a machine which must learn and which must display a measure of homeostasis. In general, methods based on the application of decision theory are suitable for use where the states of the desired signal can be exactly defind *a priori*. However, if the states of the desired signal are ill defined (e.g. speech waveforms), then filter methods are better.

In work on visual pattern recognition or character recognition, the design of the original characters is always based on the necessity for them to be recognised by a human as well as by a machine. The writer has pointed out[13] that in some cases, for example cheques, this feature is quite unnecessary; the human can read the information elsewhere on the same document.

Particularly in work on speech, it is necessary to recognise that the signals acceptable to humans are extremely redundant. The minimum standards acceptable as recognisable by a machine might be much reduced if only it was known what are the important components of a speech signal.

REFERENCES

1. ASHBY, W. R., 'Design For A Brain', *Electronic Engineering*, **V20**, 397 (1948)
2. ASHBY, W. R., *Design for a Brain*, Chapman and Hall (1952)
3. YOUNG, J. F., *Cybernetics*, Iliffe (1969)
4. YOUNG, J. F., *Information Theory*, Butterworth (1970)
5. LUTTER, B. E. and HUNTSINGER, R. C., 'Engineering Applications of Finite Automata', *Simulation*, **13**, 5 (1969)
6. STEINBUCH, K., and PISKE, U.A.W., 'Learning Matrices and their Applications', *Trans. IEEE*, **EC12**, 846 Dec. (1963)
7. SKLANSKY, J., 'Adaptation, Learning, Self repair and Feedback' *IEEE Spectrum*, **1**, 172 (1968)
8. CHOW, C. K., 'An Optimum Character Recognition System Using Decision Functions', *Trans. IRE*, **EC6**, 247 Dec. (1957)
9. GRIFFIN, J. S., KING, J. H., and TUNIS, C. J., 'Pattern Identification Using Adaptive Linear Decision Functions', *IEEE* Wescon, Paper 6.4 (1963)
10. SKLANSKY, J., 'Learning Systems for Automatic Control', *Trans. IEEE*, **AC11**, 3 (1966)
11. ROSENBLATT, F., 'Perceptron Simulation Experiments', *Proc. IRE*, **48**, 301 (1609
12. HAWKINS, J. K., 'Self-Organising Systems', *Proc. IRE* **49**, 31 (1961)
13. YOUNG, J. F., 'Cybernetics', *British Communications and Electronics*, **12**, 302 (1965)

3 | Adjustable Logic

3.1 REPRESENTATION OF HYPERSPACE

It is useful to be able to express association relationships geometrically, one reason being the ease of visualisation of the results. The representation of associations by the use of hyperspace has been widely used. In this approach,[1] the points representing different input patterns are regarded as being separated by hyperplanes which are

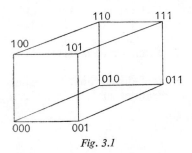

Fig. 3.1

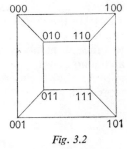

Fig. 3.2

implemented in practice by simple majority logic circuits. Unfortunately it is impossible for a human to visualise a hyperspace directly, and published representations[2] have merely used a simple two-dimensional drawing of a cube in 3-space for illustration, as shown in Figure 3.1.

It would be possible to make use of the well-known representation of a hollow hypercube for visualisation, though this fact does not seem to have been exploited. A hollow cube with binary numbered vertices can be represented in two dimensions as shown above in Figure 3.2. In a similar way, a hollow four-dimension hypercube can be represented in a two-dimensional drawing as in Figure 3.3. Thus it is quite possible, even though complex, to represent hypercubes by means of two-dimensional sketches.

17

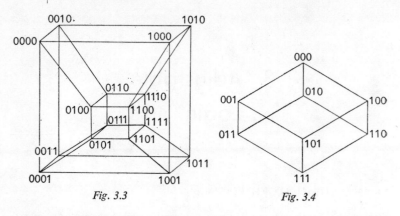

Fig. 3.3   Fig. 3.4

A useful alternative two-dimensional sketch of a 3-space representation of the associations between three inputs is shown in Figure 3.4. This gives a more logical layout of the vertices than do those of Figure 3.1.

In the first representation of Figure 3.1 the point 000 can be taken as the origin and each of the three coordinate axes is then takes as representing one of the input variables, which can each take the value 1 or 0. In the new representation of Figure 3.4 the diagram has been rotated and the layout of vertices has been changed slightly in order to bring all numbers containing the same number of binary ones to a common level.

By extending this representation, the four-dimensional hypercube representing all possible multi-way associations of four inputs can

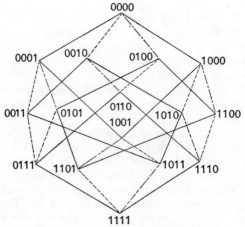

Fig. 3.5 Representation of Hypercube

be drawn in two dimensions as in Figure 3.5. Compared with the previous representation, the inner cube is now 'suspended' below the outer cube.

It will be noticed that the numbers of vertices in the different horizontal arrays are equal to the Pascal binomial coefficients, for example, 1,4,6,4,1. The total number of vertices is equal to the sum of all of the Pascal coefficients, which is in turn produced by a binary progression. For example, $1+4+6+4+1 = 16 = 2^4$. The number of connections going downwards from each vertex decreases uniformly as the digram is traversed from top to bottom, for example 4,3,2,1 in the diagram shown.

Four edges terminate at each vertex. The binary numbers of the vertices joined by any single line differ by only one digit. Every plane is common to two 3-cubes and on the diagram each 3-cube is simply represented by twelve lines. Some of the 3-cube representations are very distorted. An example has vertices:

0001-0000-1000-1001;   0011-0010-1010-1011.

Another has vertices:

0011-1011-1111-0111;   0010-1010-1110-0110.

Thus it is quite possible to represent a hypercube by a two-dimensional drawing and to use this to study the connectivities between vertices. As the number of dimensions of the hypercube increases, so the interconnections of the diagram become extremely complicated, but the layout of the vertices in two dimensions is quite straight forward.

To separate out a number of hypercube vertices for recognition, all lines on the diagram joining any required vertices to any non required vertices must be cut by the separating hyperplanes.[3] In order for it to be possible to separate out a set of points using only a single hyperplane, it must be possible to draw along the lines of the diagram which pass through all points of the required set, a joining line which does not pass through any other points which are not in the set. The separating hyperplane must then pass through all of those other lines of the diagram which connect points of the required set to points which are non members of the set. If it is not possible to draw such an exclusive joining line, then more than one hyperplane is required for the separation. As a simple illustration of this, two separate intersecting planes would be required to obtain the function $A(Bc+bC)$ in three dimensions, i.e. to separate out the points 101 and 110. On the other hand, only one plane is required for the function $A(B+C)$, which involves the separation out of the points 101, 110, and 111.

It might be convenient to study the surface formed by joining the mid-points of those lines which connect points which must be separated, e.g. the mid-point of the line joining vertex 101 to vertex 100 in the last example. If necessary, the nature of this surface could be investigated by comparison with the various planes joining the vertices. The effect of a threshold change in a majority logic gate is to move the corresponding hyperplane vertically, while independent changes of individual coefficients rotate the hyperplane.

3.2 GEOMETRIC REPRESENTATION OF ASSOCIATIONS

It is useful to be able to visualise the principle of operation of a machine. In some of the published work on character-recognition, for example, every possible set of conditions of the N inputs has been represented by a different vector from a set in N-dimensional space[4] as described above.

In the present work, consideration is given to associations between pairs of inputs. If each input is represented by a point, then the possible associations between inputs can be represented by lines joining

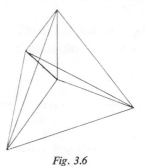

Fig. 3.6

the points. For two inputs, A and B, a single straight line represents the association AB. For three inputs A, B, C a triangle AB, BC, CA, is required. The six possible two-way associations between four inputs are represented by a pyramid, each side being an equilateral triangle. To represent the ten possible two-way associations between five inputs, a four-dimensional hyperpyramid is required. A three-dimensional sketch model looking 'inside' such a hyperpyramid is shown in Figure 3.6. On the model, as on any drawing, the distances are distorted.

Now if more than five inputs are to be represented, figures in a multidimensional space are required. It was realised that any of these could be sketched, with distance-distortion, in three dimensions. This in turn led to a two-dimensional distorted representation.

It is convenient to have all input points A, B, C... equispaced around a circle as in Figure 3.7 and to represent the associations

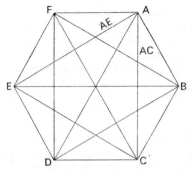

Fig. 3.7 Representation of associations

between inputs by straight lines. The thickness or number of straight lines joining any two input points can then be used to indicate the strength of the association between these points.

This method of representation illustrates clearly that the greater the number of inputs, the more difficult becomes the problem of distinguishing one association from another. The arbitrary assumption of orthogonality often used[5] implies that each situation is completely separable from any other situation.

The real justification for the use of orthogonal representation is that it places every situation near to every other situation. This is also true of the simplified method of representation of two-way associations given here, and the representation can easily be drawn or visualised for any number of inputs.

3.3 SEQUENTIAL STIMULI

It is an open question whether or not there is any form of direct storage in the human and animal nervous system of the nature of the time-sequence of the stimuli being detected by the sensors. While it is natural to assume that there must be, it is difficult to know what form it could take.

There is no doubt that any nerve fibre can be considered as being in effect a delay line, and various people have suggested how a number of such delay lines could produce a form of sequence-sensitivity in the nervous system. This form could easily be built into a robot mechanism by the use of electrical or pneumatic delay lines having a number of tappings, each of which provides an output from the line. These delayed outputs can then be associated with any inputs appearing at a slightly later time.

In many cases there will in any case be an overlap in time between the various stimuli, and it may be that the animal nervous system simply makes use of this.

It is of interest to consider how time-order affects the operation of a machine in which a certain time-integral of excitation was required in order to produce a particular output. Suppose that associations *X*, *Y*, *Z* occur in succession and that each produces a certain integral of excitation of a particular output. Suppose that *X*, *Y*, *Z*, correspond to inputs *AB*, *BC*, *CD*, i.e. that the inputs *A*, *B*, *C*, *D*, have appeared with overlap in time. Now if the inputs appear with *D* out of sequence as *ADBC*, then only the association *Y* = *BC* appears. The time-integral of excitation of the output in question is consequently much lower than it would be if the inputs appeared in the order *ABCD*.

This approach demonstrates that there is some probability of obtaining sequence-sensitivity merely by use of a simple threshold arrangement at the output, combined with a time-integration of output stimuli.

Now with such a system, some ambiguity is inherent, since a sequence and its inverse (e.g. *ABCD* and *DCBA*) produce the same result. It is interesting to note that in the absence of other clues, this is just the form of presentation of information which appears to cause the greatest ambiguity to a human observer.

Although the human being in his normal environment appears to have a very good time-sensitivity, even when asleep, the sensitivity is lost completely in experiments involving sensory deprivation. Consequently, it may be that human time-sensitivity is accomplished entirely by association with external stimuli. It is possible that some at least of the sensory sequence-sensitivity[6] is accomplished in a similar way.

3.4 THE ASTON DEMONSTRATION PERCEPTRON

In order to be able to demonstrate to students the basic method used in many different forms of perceptron-type of device, Starmer's form of majority logic circuit is used at Aston. This was designed and built as a student project. All of the input resistors are adjustable, and this adjustment constitutes the 'training' of the device. One easy demonstration of the basic simplicity of the perceptron process is shown in Figure 3.8.

A square matrix is constructed from nine photoelectric cells of the cadmium sulphide type. Each of the cells is connected to an input of the adjustable majority-logic circuit via an emitter follower as shown in Figure 3.8.

In order to distinguish between X and Y placed before the matrix of photo-cells, the corresponding input resistors are adjusted to the relative values shown in brackets. These are the weight adjustments

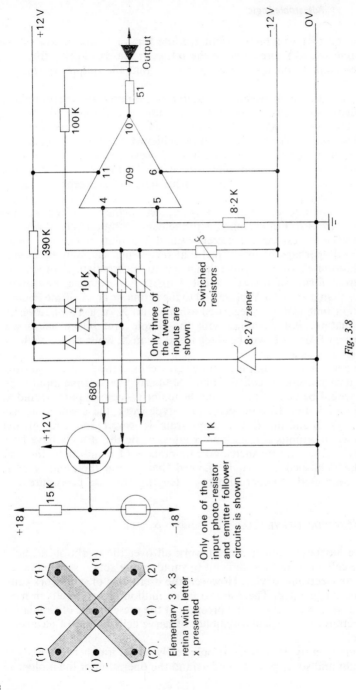

Fig. 3.8

required to give a high output reading for an X and a low output reading for a Y presented to the retina or matrix of cells. It is easy, if required, to change these settings so that the output operation is inverted.

Where the input weight is required to be unity, the corresponding input resistor value is set at 10 000 ohms. For a weight of two the resistor is set to 5000 ohms and for a weight of three the resistor is set to 3300 ohms. These values can be achieved if required by following a setting-up (or training) procedure. However, there seems to be no reason why, if a human operator (or teacher) is required at all, he should not make use of a little of his human intelligence in setting up the machine.

As the number of inputs used is increased, so the difficulty of setting-up is increased. For example, with the demonstration unit shown, the difference in resistance between 19 and 20 inputs is only 20 ohms. It should perhaps be mentioned that such a unit can only be used to 'dichotomise', or in simpler language to differentiate between two different forms of object presented to it. For example, any object other than an X or a Y presented to the retina or array of the demonstration unit will be categorised as either an X or a Y, whatever its true nature. For example, with the simple unit set-up as shown, either an F or an L will be categorised as an X, while an O would be categorised as a Y.

In perceptron terms, the photo-electric cells in the Aston demonstration device would be called S units. Similarly, the variable input resistors would be called A units and the majority-logic amplifer would be called an R unit. In some perceptron-type work, the connections between the S and the R units are 'scramble' wired, and a far greater number of A units is used than S units, while the A units have been interwired to give an increased randomness of connection. In some of the published work it is claimed that several thousand A units have been used, together with a very lengthy 'training' procedure.

3.5 ARTIFICIAL NERVE CELLS

There has been a great deal of work all over the world on artificial nerve cells. It is not too difficult to simulate the action of a nerve cell with an electronic device. However, the usefulness of such work must not be exaggerated. There are so many million of nerve cells in most organisms, that there is little prospect at the present time of simulating the action of biological assemblies of nerve cells by use of electronic models.

Consequently, such work is only really useful if either it stimulates thought and so helps us to understand the operation of the biological nervous system, or if the work leads to devices which might be useful in other applications. There are many examples of work in the first category.

In the second category, there has been much work on so-called Majority Logic arrangements. A nerve cell has a number of inputs and one main output. It appears to have the property that when more than a certain given number of the inputs are stimulated electrically, then an electrical output is given.

Such a device would be of great use in work on digital computers for two reasons. Firstly, it is possible that the use of these majority logic circuits might have the effect of reducing the cost and the size of digital computers. Secondly, and perhaps more important at the present time, such circuitry might help to increase the speed of operation of digital computers.

It is interest to consider the reason for the latter property, since this is an example of cybernetic engineering—the application to engineering of devices and techniques derived from biology.

A single majority logic circuit can be used to replace a number of the more usual binary logic circuits in a computer. As a simple example, suppose that it is required to obtain an output from a logic circuit whenever two or more of the inputs are energised. If there happen to be a maximum of four possible inputs, A, B, C, D, then the requirement can be stated as:

$$\text{Output} = A.B + A.C + A.D + B.C + B.D + C.D$$

It can be seen from this that the embodiment of this arrangement using normal logical circuits requires the use of six two-way AND gates with one five-way OR gate. It is possible to reduce the number of gates required in various ways. However, to meet the same requirement using majority logic circuits requires the use of only one two-or-more majority logic gate. The cost and the size of the equipment is therefore likely to be reduced.

Perhaps more important, since only one gate is required, there is only one basic delay, compared with the minimum of two basic units of delay in the minimum of two stages of logic used with normal circuitry. Any attempt to achieve economy with the normal logic circuitry is likely to increase the delay still further. Thus majority logic, which is one form of simulation of neural logic, is likely to have a future in the field of digital computers as well as in cybernetic engineering.

There is a most important point in connection with work on majority logic which should be stressed. Many workers have stated that a unit should emit a signal whenever the total summated signal to the input exceeds a certain fixed value. This form can be regarded as a fixed threshold form of majority logic.

However, if there are several units, then it is possible to arrange that only that unit which has the greatest total summated input signals should emit an output signal. In effect, this provides a variable form of threshold logic which selects the most important and urgent unit, and produces an output based on signal urgency.

In the biological case, a choice must be made of which muscle or muscles are to be actuated in any particular circumstances, and this can only be done on a Maximum-Majority basis. Ambiguity of action cannot be accepted. However, if by following this process the wrong action is chosen, then the input situation will change very rapidly and the correct action will follow. In effect, this involves a form of feedback of the results of any action.

REFERENCES

1. HIGHLEYMAN, W. H., 'Linear Decision Functions, With Application to Pattern Recognition', *Proc. IRE*, **50**, 1501 (1962)
2. HAWKINS, J. K. 'Self-Organising Systems', *Proc. IRE*, **49**, 31 (1961)
3. GRIFFIN, J. S., KING, J. H., and TUNIS, C. J., 'Pattern Identification Using Adaptive Linear Decision Functions', *IEEE* Wescon, Paper 6.4 (1963)
4. STEINBUCH, K., and PISKE, U. A. W., 'Learning Matrices and their Applications', *Trans. IEEE*, **EC12**, 846 (1963)
5. NAGY, G., 'State of the Art in Pattern Recognition', *Proc. IEEE*, **56**, 836 (1968)
6. SCOTT, P., and WILLIAMS, K. G., 'A Note on Temporal Coding as a Mechanism in Sensory Perception', *Inf. Control*, **2**, 380 (1959)

4 | Majority Logic

In some work, the various inputs to a logic circuit are considered to have variable values. This is accomplished either by variation of the amplitude of the input voltage or by variation of the magnitude of the individual input resistors.

The treatment of multi-input logic circuits can be simplified by first considering all of the inputs to have equal amplitudes of voltage and circuit impedance. Only the number energised or de-energised is then considered. As will be seen later, such an approach is valuable when the application of majority logic circuits to the simplification and speeding of binary digital computer circuits is considered.

The consideration can be extended later if required to the variable amplitude case by considering the variation of amplitude to be equivalent to a change of the number of inputs energised or to the number of input circuit impedances connected to an individual input source.

In this way, the binary approach can be generalised if required. However, in much of the work at the present stage the generalisation is not necessary. It is possible to show, as will be seen later, that the voltage tolerance is very important in these circuits, and if the binary approach can be used then it is possible to standardise the input amplitudes using Zener diodes and so obtain an improved reliability.

4.1 RELAY MAJORITY LOGIC

Majority-logic circuits using electro-mechanical relays are well-known. An example devised by the writer for use in numerical-control equipment for machine tools is shown in Figure 4.1. One of the output terminals is energised whenever an even number of input relays is energised. Circuits such as this can be regarded as degenerate form of the complete relay contact circuit shown in Figure 4.2.

A two-or-more circuit derived from the complete arrangement

27

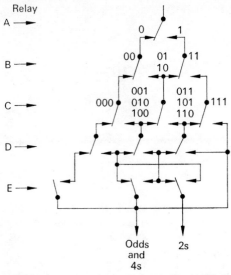

Fig. 4.1 Punched-tape parity checking circuit for machine-tool control

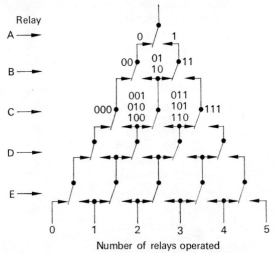

Fig. 4.2 Complete number-routing circuit

requires a maximum of two change-over contacts on each relay. A slight reduction of the contact requirements would be obtained by using complementary circuitry, i.e. by building a relay-contact 0 or 1 circuit and then inverting the output. The relay contact arrangement is shown for six relay inputs in Figure 4.3.

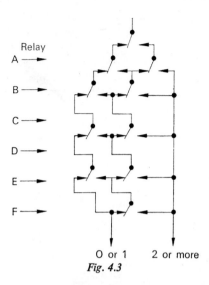

O or 1   2 or more
Fig. 4.3

Solid-state relays could be used to increase the speed of action of these circuits. At present, this approach would be quite expensive. However it is hoped that integrated forms of these circuits will become available in the future.

4.2 RESISTIVE MAJORITY LOGIC

There are two basic methods of achieving a circuit which gives an output signal whenever two or more input terminals are stimulated simultaneously. One uses binary logical AND gates and this approach is described later.

The alternative approach requires less equipment, but there are difficulties in obtaining reliability. This method is sometimes called

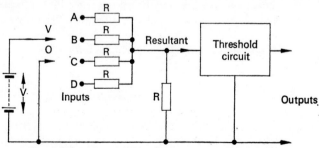

Fig. 4.4 Resistive majority logic using analogue addition

'Analogue Addition,' and the basis is illustrated by the circuit shown in Figure 4.4.

Suppose that each of the inputs A, B, C, D in Figure 4.4 can be connected either to a voltage V or to a zero voltage 0. The relationships between the input voltages to terminals A, B, C, D and the output voltage across the common shunt resistor are given in Table 4.1

Table 4.1

A	B	C	D	*Output*
0	0	0	0	0
0	0	0	V	0·2 V
0	0	V	0	0·2 V
0	0	V	V	0·4 V
0	V	0	0	0·2 V
0	V	0	V	0·4 V
0	V	V	0	0·4 V
0	V	V	V	0·6 V
V	0	0	0	0·2 V
V	0	0	V	0·4 V
V	0	V	0	0·4 V
V	0	V	V	0·6 V
V	V	0	0	0·4 V
V	V	0	V	0·6 V
V	V	V	0	0·6 V
V	V	V	V	0·8 V

From Table 4.1, it can be seen that if the threshold circuit is designed to give an output only if the resultant voltage exceeds 0·3 V, then the output provides the logical indication of:

$$V_0 = A.B + A.C + A.D + B.C + B.D + C.D \qquad (4.1)$$

An output is therefore obtained only if two or more inputs are present.

For a general $(N-1)$ input circuit of this type, the outputs are:

Number of inputs stimulated	*Output voltage*
0	0
1	$V.1/N$
2	$V.2/N$
3	$V.3/N$
......	....
$N-1$	$V.(1-1/N)$

Thus in order to detect the difference between the stimulation of X inputs and the stimulation of $(X+1)$ inputs, the threshold circuit must differentiate between voltages which only differ by V/N. This becomes an increasingly difficult practical task as the value of N increases.[2]

In the above it has been assumed that all resistors have equal values. However, suppose that the output shunt resistor has a value R_p instead of R. Then if X inputs are stimulated, the output becomes:

$$V_0 = V\left(\frac{X}{R/R_p+N-1}\right) \tag{4.2}$$

It follows that the threshold circuit is now required to differentiate between voltages differing by:

$$\frac{V}{R/R_p+N-1} \tag{4.3}$$

The curves in Figure 4.5 show the variation of this fractional voltage threshold for various values of N.

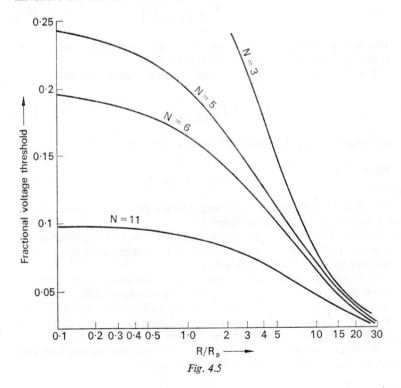

Fig. 4.5

From Figure 4.5, it is seen to be advantageous if $R_p > R$. However there is not much gain beyond the value $R_p = 2R$.

Suppose now that the circuit is changed so that in the absence of an input excitation, an input resistor is open-circuited instead of being connected down to the zero line. Then with equal-valued input resistors the outputs become:

Number of inputs stimulated	Output voltage
0	0
1	V.1/2
2	V.2/3
3	V.3/4
4	V.4/5
......	....
$N-1$	$V(1-1/N)$

If the output resistor has a value R_p and the number of inputs stimulated is X, then the output is:

$$V_0 = V\left(\frac{1}{R/XR_p+1}\right) \tag{4.4}$$

The way in which this function varies with the resistor ratio R/R_p is shown in Figure 4.6 for various values of X.

If now $X+1$ inputs are stimulated, then the output becomes:

$$V_0 = V\left(\frac{1}{R/(X+1)R_p+1}\right) \tag{4.5}$$

Consequently the threshold difference to be detected is:

$$\text{Threshold difference} = V\left(\frac{R/R_p}{(R/R_p+X)(R/R_p+X+1)}\right) \tag{4.6}$$

This threshold difference function is plotted against the value of R/R_p for various values of X in Figure 4.7.

It should be noted that the threshold level depends in value on the number X of inputs to be stimulated, but not necessarily on the total number $(N-1)$ of inputs connected.

With any of the methods described in this section, it is seen that for more than about ten inputs, the fractional voltage difference to be detected becomes rather small. Consequently, such circuits having a voltage-operated output could not be expected to give a good reliability if used with a large number of inputs.

A better performance can be obtained with the current-operated circuits to be described in the following sections.

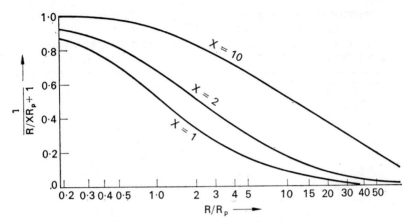

Fig. 4.6 Variation of output with ratio of resistors

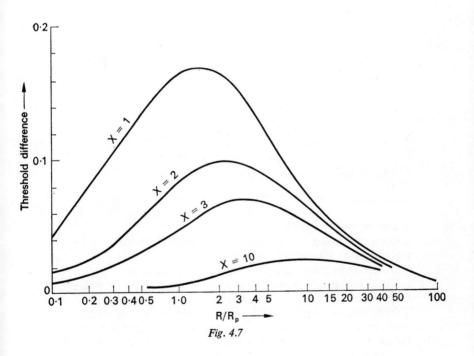

Fig. 4.7

4.3 RESISTOR-TRANSISTOR CIRCUITS

The form of logical switching circuit incorporating a transistor with a number of base input resistors is well known, and has been widely used. It is often known as a *NOR* circuit, though other designations have been used. The principles and equations of operation of such circuits are well known.

A resistor-transistor *NOR* circuit which uses a *PNP* type of transistor is referred to in the terminology originated by the writer as a 'Positive output for One Negative input' circuit, or simply as a *PIN* circuit.[3] This form of designation has been shown to have the advantage that it completely eliminates the usual confusion which is commonly caused by indiscriminate use of the term *NOR*.

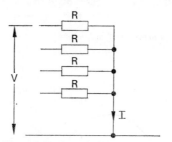

Fig. 4.8 Basic resistor arrangement

It is possible to design such circuits so that they require two or more of the inputs to be energised before an output is given, and the writer has introduced the designation *P2N* for such 'Two-or-More' circuits. An alternative brief designation for this type of circuit in the general case, where no reference can be made to a specific polarity of semiconductor, can be derived by analogy with the term *NOR*. It is *TOR*, standing for 'Two-Or-More' circuit, and this designation is convenient to use in the present case.

It will be shown later how either a general majority logic circuit or a 'Perceptron' type of circuit can be derived quite simply by the addition of an extra bias input to a two-or-more circuit.

The operation of the resistor-transistor *TOR* circuit is based on the property of the simple resistor arrangement illustrated in Figure 4.8. If the voltage applied to each input is zero when the input is unstimulated and is V when the input is stimulated, then with a number X of stimulated inputs, the output current is equal to XV/R. The dependence of output current on the number X of stimulated inputs is therefore linear.

The change of output current per added input is therefore V/R and is independent of the actual number X of inputs stimulated.

To construct a two-or-more circuit on this basis, it is necessary to detect a current of $2V/R$ or greater and to ignore currents of V/R or less. The detection threshold should therefore be set at $1\cdot5V/R$.

For the complete resistor-transistor TOR circuit of Figure 4.9 two conditions of operation must be fulfilled. When two inputs are simultaneously stimulated with voltage V, the transistor must carry base current I_b so that the collector conducts and the output terminal is moved positively. This requirement is expressed by equation (4.7),

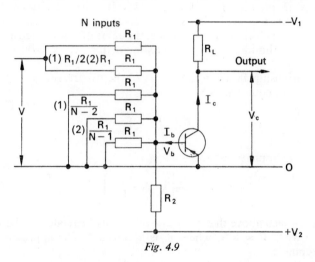

Fig. 4.9

where V_{b-} is the base-to-emitter voltage of the transistor when it is carrying base current I_b (and so conducting in the collector circuit), and N is the total number of inputs.

$$\frac{V-V_{b-}}{R_1/2} = \frac{V_{b-}(N-2)}{R_1} + I_b + \frac{V_2+V_{b-}}{R_2} \qquad (4.7)$$

When only one input is energised with voltage V, the transistor is required to be cut off with its base positive to its emitter by voltage V_{b+}. Its collector then only carries the low reverse leakage current I_{c0}:

$$\frac{V+V_{b+}}{R_1} + \frac{V_{b+}(N-1)}{R_1} + I_{c0} = \frac{V-V_{b+}}{R_2} \qquad (4.8)$$

From these equations, the required value of R_1 is

$$R_1 = \frac{(V_2-V_{b+})(2V-NV_{b-})-(V_2+V_{b-})(V+NV_{b+})}{I_{c0}(V_2+V_{b-})+I_b(V_2-V_{b+})} \qquad (4.9)$$

As an approximation, if $V_{b+} \ll V_2$, $V_{b-} \ll V_2$ and I_{c0} is small, then:

$$R_1 = \frac{V - N(V_{b-} + V_{b+})}{I_b} \quad (4.10)$$

Hence it is necessary to have

$$V > N(V_{b-} + V_{b+}) \quad (4.11)$$

and since in practice $V_{b-} + V_{b+} \not> 1/4$ volts, then the basic design requirement is $V > N/4$. This gives a remarkably simple approach to the design of such circuits. In practice, the value of V is limited and this fact places a limitation on the maximum number of inputs which can be used.

The relationship between the values of the two resistors R_1 and R_2 is found from equation (4.8):

$$R_2 = R_1 \left[\frac{V - V_{b+}}{V + N V_{b+}} \right] \quad (4.12)$$

Hence as an approximation:

$$R_1 \approx R_2 \left[1 + N \frac{V_{b+}}{V} \right] \quad (4.13)$$

It has been seen above that the value of V must be related to the value of N, so write $V = KN$, where K is a constant. The approximation then becomes:

$$R_1 \approx R_2 \left[1 + \frac{V_{b+}}{K} \right] \quad (4.14)$$

Equations (4.7) to (4.14) give a guide to the practical design of *TOR* cicuits using transistors and resistors, though it is difficult to fix the values of V_{b+} and V_{b-}.

The minimum permissible value of collector load resistor R_L is determined by two factors. First, the base current must be sufficient to bottom the transistor. Secondly it is desirable to limit the maximum possible collector dissipation W_m of the transistor. Now the collector voltage is given by:

$$V_c = V_1 - I_c R_L \quad (4.15)$$

Whence, by differentiation, $W^m = V_1^2/4R_L$. The design requirement[4] is therefore

$$R_L \geqslant \frac{V_1^2}{4W_m} \quad (4.15)$$

4.4 INTEGRATED-AMPLIFIER TOR CIRCUIT

Equation (4.11) shows that the number of inputs which can be used with a resistor-transistor *TOR* circuit is less than

$$N < \frac{V}{V_{b-} + V_{b+}} \qquad (4.16)$$

This can be written as:

$$N < \frac{V}{V_p} \qquad (4.17)$$

where V_p is the smallest range over which the input base-to-emitter voltage of the transistor must swing in order to change the state of the transistor from the fully-on to the fully-off condition. Consequently, the smaller the required base-to-emitter input voltage swing required, the greater the number N of inputs which can be used. Now the required voltage swing is a function of the voltage gain of the transistor used.

Integrated amplifiers having a high voltage gain have recently become available at low cost. The possibility therefore occurs of using one of these to replace the amplifying transistor in a *TOR* circuit. The possibility was tried out using an integrated amplifier type SL701c.

The basic circuit is as shown in Figure 4.10. If it is assumed that the range of amplifier input voltage swing required is very much less than either V or the maximum positive or negative values of V_0, then analysis of the arrangement shows that:

$$\frac{2V_0}{R_3} = \frac{V - V_b(2N-3)}{R_1} \qquad (4.18)$$

where N is the number of inputs and V_b is approximately one half of the required input voltage swing. Also, $V_0 \approx V$. It follows that it is necessary to have

$$V > V_b(2N-3). \qquad (4.19)$$

Now $V/V_b \approx A$, and if $N > 1$ then $N \gg A/2$. This means that, since A is large, majority logic circuits having very many inputs can be constructed.

Using the SL701c amplifier shown in Figure 4.11, it was quite possible to handle 100 inputs and to obtain reliable two-or-more operation. No attempt was made to obtain the ultimate performance in these tests, since it was never necessary to work with more than twenty inputs in the initial work. Moreover, the design of integrated

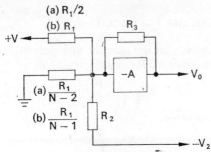

Fig. 4.10 *Integrated-amplifier TOR circuit*

amplifiers is progressing continuously at the present time, while the cost is falling rapidly.

In the writer's terminology,[3] the circuit of Figure 4.11 is called an *N2P* circuit. With arrangements such as this, the writer's students have carried out preliminary work on pulse-height standardisation by use of a Zener diode in each input circuit of a *TOR* arrangement.

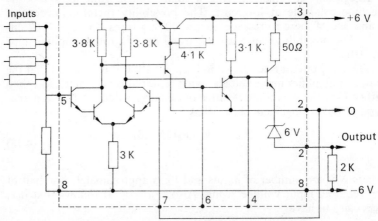

Fig. 4.11 *SL701c Integrated amplifier in TOR circuit*

4.5 INHIBITORY INPUTS TO TOR CIRCUITS

With the *TOR* arrangement described earlier, all input voltages are equal to either 0 or $+V$. A negative output is obtained when there are two-or-more positive inputs. It is possible to make some of the inputs inhibitory by connecting them to an input voltage of $-V$. We simply put $-V_2 = -V$, and $R_2 = R_1/M$ in Figure 4.10, while we have L

inputs connected to voltage $+V$ and $N-M-L$ inputs connected to ground. In these circumstances, if the gain A is large so that V_b is small then if $L = M-1$, the output voltage is $V_0 = VR_3/R_1$; if $L = M$, the output voltage is $V_0 = 0$; and if $L = M+1$, the output voltage is $V_0 = -VR_3/R_1$.

It is convenient to set an output threshold voltage of $-VR_3/2R_1$, an output being indicated if the voltage is more negative than this value. In this case, an output is obtained if $L \geqslant M+1$. If only a single resistor $R_2 = R_1$ is fitted as in the earlier case, then $M = 1$ and the arrangement becomes a two-or-more circuit which gives a negative output voltage if ever the number of inputs L taken to a positive supply exceeds two.

4.6 TOR CIRCUIT COMPONENT AND VOLTAGE TOLERANCES

It is here convenient to consider the input conductances rather than the resistances. In the TOR input circuit shown in Figure 4.12, suppose that the fractional tolerance on each conductance is g, so that the

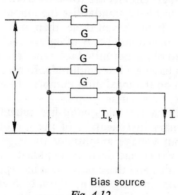

Bias source

Fig. 4.12

value of each conductance lies in the range $(1 \pm g)G$. Also suppose that the actual tolerance on each input voltage is v, so that the value of each input voltage lies in the range $(V \pm v)$. Also let the voltage tolerance on each input which is nominally grounded also be v, so that a 'ground' point is actually at a voltage in the range $\pm v$.

Then the maximum input current with only one input is:

$$I_{max\,1} = (V+v)(1+g)G+(N-1)v(1+g)G-I_k \qquad (4.20)$$

while the minimum input current with two inputs is:

$$I_{min\,2} = 2(V-v)(1-g)G-(N-2)v(1+g)G-I_k \qquad (4.21)$$

Here N is the total number of inputs and I_k is the constant bias current. It is necessary to ensure that

$$I_{\min 2} > I_{\max 1} \qquad (4.22)$$

From these relationships, the maximum number of inputs is given by:

$$N < \frac{V/v+g}{2(1+g)} \approx \frac{V}{2v} \qquad (4.23)$$

since g is small. Thus under the conditions stated, the maximum number of inputs is determined mainly by the voltage tolerance.

4.7 INPUT STANDARDISATION

Various practical forms of the majority logic circuits discussed above have been investigated by the writer's students at Aston. For example, Fisher and Russell have investigated the use of early low-cost minia-ture D.C. amplifiers and of low-cost integrated circuit D.C. amplifiers in majority logic circuitry for pulse applications.

Now if majority logic circuits are to be used with large numbers of inputs, it will be desirable to standardise the amplitudes of the inputs as much as possible. If this is not done, then as has been seen it will be difficult to distinguish a number N of inputs, each having an ampli-tude at the upper end of the permitted tolerance range, from a number $N+1$ of inputs each having a low amplitude. In practice, this fact pro-vides one limitation on the maximum number of inputs which can be used with a majority logic circuit.

Some years ago the writer and one of his students, Bowen, carried out a brief preliminary investigation of the use of Zener diodes to standardise the input voltage amplitudes to majority logic circuits. More recently, the writer has devised simplified and more economic standardisation circuits, and these have been incorporated in practical majority logic circuitry investigated at Aston by Starmer.

As shown in the circuit diagram of Figure 3.8, a single integrated-circuit D.C. amplifier is used, with negative feedback from output to input. There are 20 signal inputs in all, each of which can have a posi-tive value or can be equal to zero. Following on the earlier work, each of the inputs is standardised, the maximum value of each input voltage being limited by clamping with a diode to a constant voltage source provided by a Zener diode.

The effects of the inputs are opposed by a threshold level control, consisting of a switched adjustable value resistor. In practice, this resistor is switched, to a value depending on the threshold level re-quired, by a multi-way switch mounted on the front panel of the unit.

A useful by-product of the cybernetics work at Aston is the application of the majority logic form of circuit in the possible simplification of digital computer arrangements. The basic limitation on the speed of operation of a digital computer is provided by the speed of light, since it is impossible for information to travel at a faster rate from one point of the computer to another. In order to speed-up the action of a computer, it is necessary ultimately to limit the distances through which information must travel. One way of achieving this is by limiting the number of different stages of separate logic circuitry through which the information must pass, and the use of majority logic has this effect.

There is another reason, besides distance, for wishing to limit the number of stages. Each stage introduces a switching delay, due for example to the switching time of semiconductors. Again, the delay is reduced by a limitation of the number of different stages, and again majority logic has this effect. Consequently some of the students who have worked on this at Aston are financed by computer manufacturers.

4.8 DIODE MAJORITY LOGIC

In the course of preliminary work, it is sometimes convenient to use diode logic circuitry to carry out the required majority logic operations, since the diodes can easily be plugged in the required positions on a diode matrix by use of a special plug-board. As an example, with a simple four-input two-or-more majority logic circuit, the required operation is:

$$A.B + A.C + A.D + B.C + B.D + C.D$$

To carry out such an operation with N inputs, a total of $\frac{1}{2}.N(N-1)$ AND gates is required. Each AND gate must have two input diodes, and each is followed by a diode which forms part of an output OR gate. Consequently, to implement this approach, a total of $\frac{3}{2}.N(N-1)$ diodes is required. It follows that the number of diodes required increases very rapidly as the number of input circuits is increased.

While this approach is consequently not practicable for use with a large number of inputs, it is convenient for any initial work where majority logic will be required.

REFERENCES

1. DERTOUZOS, M. L., *Threshold Logic*, M.I.T. (1965)
2. TAYLOR, W. K.,'Pattern Recognition by means of Automatic Analogue Apparatus', *Proc. IEE*, **106B**, 198 (1959)
3. YOUNG, J. F., 'Variable Polarity Logic', *Control* **9**, 493 (1965)
4. YOUNG, J. F., *Applied Electronics*, Iliffe (1968)

5 | Neural Activity

A very simple form of artificial nerve cell produced by the writer in 1951 is shown in Figure 5.1. When an input voltage pulse is applied, the capacitor C_3 is charged and the circuit begins to produce output pulses, the shape of the pulses depending on the resonant frequency and on the value of the Q-factor of the resonant circuit at the output.

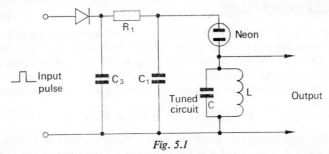

Fig. 5.1

This arrangement provides a short-term memory of excitation. Since the output pulse can take the form of a resonant 'ringing' at the frequency of the tuned circuit, it is possible to associate the operation of a number of such nerve cells in a sinusoidal type of association-recording machine. The chief virtue of this arrangement lies in its simplicity. Other bistable elements, such as solid-state forms, can be used to replace the neon tube used in the early experiments.

5.2 NEURON ASSEMBLIES

Numbers of people have been attracted to work on the properties of assemblies of neurons. In much of this work the false assumption appears to have been made implicitly that the nervous system consists of a flat, two dimensional, array of cells. It is natural to try to reduce the problem in this way, since the average human being finds it much easier to think about numbers of objects in two dimensions rather than three, and visualisation of a three dimensional array is difficult. However, this severely restricts the practical utility of such work.

Because of this difficulty, only a limited amount of work on neuron assemblies has been carried out at Aston. However, one point of great interest has received attention. This is the mysterious rhythmic electrical activity of the cortex of the human brain.

The surface of part of the human brain exhibits a continuous state of electrical oscillation, one type of waveform produced being known as the Alpha Rhythm. This rhythmic activity proves to be very useful for medical diagnostic purposes. However, the reason for the existence of the alpha rhythm has been rather a mystery. Various theories have been put forward in an attempt to explain the electrical waveform, but all have appeared to involve some basic difficulty.

The theory of alpha rhythm production which has been evolved at Aston is based on observation of the cell structure of the cortex of man. When stained in such a way that the nuclei of the brain cells are visible, it is seen by looking along the surface of certain microphotographs in a particular direction that the cells are arranged in remarkably straight lines.

Such a structure leads to a simple simulatory model, based on the well-known neon-tube relaxation oscillator, as shown in Figure 5.2. Here, a number of devices such as neon tubes, having non linear electrical characteristics, are connected in a series string. A capacitor is connected across the whole string. The capacitor is charged via a constant-current generator, a valve being used in the demonstration equipment as shown.

The capacitor charging current I is almost constant in value regardless of the instantaneous value V of the voltage across the capacitor. Consequently, the capacitor voltage V is equal to:

$$V = \frac{Q}{C} = \frac{1}{C} \int I \, dt$$

where Q is the electrical charge on the capacitor (Coulombs)
C is the capacitance value (Farads)

From this, if the current I is constant in value:

$$V = \frac{It}{C}$$

and the voltage V across the capacitor increases linearly with time t.

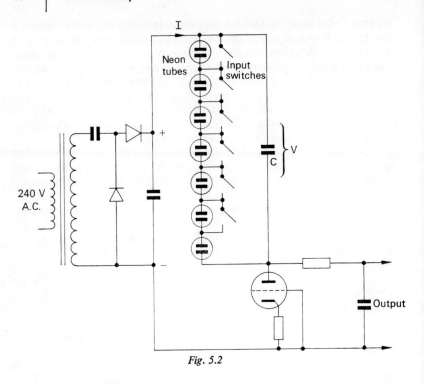

Fig. 5.2

5.3 RHYTHMIC ACTIVITY

Now if there is a total number N of neon tubes in series and if each one fires at a peak voltage value V_p, then the maximum voltage across the capacitor must be equal to $NV_p = V_M$. Also, if each of the N neon tubes extinguishes when the voltage across it is equal to a value V_e, then the minimum voltage across the capacitor must be equal to $NV_e = V_m$.

The time required to charge the capacitor from its minimum voltage V_m to its maximum voltage V_M is then given by:

$$V_M - V_m = N(V_p - V_e) = \frac{It}{C}$$

or

$$t = \frac{CN(V_p - V_e)}{I}$$

Thus if the values of C, V_p, V_e and I are all constant, then the time t must be linearly dependent on the number N of tubes in series.

If some of the neon tubes are fired prematurely, or if they are shorted out by the input switches shown, then effectively the value of N is reduced and the value t of the period of oscillation also reduced. Consequently the value f of the frequency of oscillation is increased:

$$f = \frac{1}{t} = \frac{I}{CN(V_p - V_e)}$$

Now the alpha rhythmic activity of the brain appears to have the property that the greater the number of neural inputs to the cortex, the greater the frequency of rhythmic electrical oscillation. In addition, the greater the number of inputs the lower the amplitude of the rhythmic activity of the cortex. This feature is also produced by the analogous circuit.

If the cells of the cortex of the brain had the non linear electrical characteristics similar to those possessed by a neon tube, then it would be possible to explain some of the rhythmic properties of the human brain in terms of a neural circuitry similar to that of the electronic circuits of Figure 5.2.

However, to achieve such an explanation, it is necessary not only to examine more carefully the possible linear structure of cortical cell assemblies. It is first necessary also to show that it is possible at all for electrolytic devices, such as cortical cells, to have non linear peaked electrical characteristics similar in shape to those of neon tubes.

A possible mechanism is in fact found as an interface effect in electrolytes, and the effect appears to be caused mainly by the oxygen dissolved in the electrolytic liquid. In fact the effect is often known as the 'Oxygen Peak'. Now this is a remarkable coincidence, because the whole of the activity of the brain, and indeed of the nervous system, is believed to depend critically on the amount of oxygen which is dissolved in the blood and which is available for use in nervous activity. If the oxygen is missing, the brain simply ceases to function. The individual loses consciousness and dies. The brain is not itself capable of detecting a shortage of dissolved oxygen at all, and taking corrective action.

Thus, while it cannot be claimed that the circuit shown is a true analogue of rhythmic brain activity, the coincidences are somewhat remarkable.

5.4 NEURAL PROPAGATION

It is possible to simulate some of the known features of the propagation of information in the nervous system, making use of various forms of electronic circuitry. It is therefore of use at this point to summarise some of the known features of neural propagation.

A nerve fibre passes signals on an all-or-nothing basis. The neural sheath is normally non conducting. When the sheath does conduct, it does so for only a short time, of the order of a millisecond only. Then it recovers to the non conducting state. Any in-between condition of partial conduction can persist for a very short time only. Information is conveyed along nerve fibres by such transients in a form of pulse-frequency-modulation.

The nerve fibre[1] has very special properties which make its action unlike that of an electrical passive transmission line. The form of the propagating nervous signal depends only on the nature of the nerve fibre and not on the means by which the signal is started. After an impulse has passed any given point on the nerve fibre, a short recovery (or refractory) time is required before the next impulse can pass.

If separate impulses start from opposite ends of a fibre, they are mutually destructive when they meet or collide, since each leaves behind it a refractory region through which neither impulse can continue to propagate. There can be no reflection of a signal when it reaches the end of a neural transmission line, because of the refractory region behind it.

Biological nerve fibres convey information by means of pulse-frequency-modulation. The greater the excitation intensity E, the greater the frequency of the pulses produced. Let I be the (constant valued) intensity of a single impulse and let f be the rate or frequency of the impulses. Then we can write:

$$E = If \tag{5.1}$$

Now a neuron produces impulses when it is stimulated by some external stimulus S, provided that the stimulus S exceeds a certain threshold intensity i. As a first approximation we can write:

$$f = K_1(S-i) \tag{5.2}$$

where K_1 is a constant. Hence:

$$E = IK_1(S-i) \tag{5.3}$$

$$E = K(S-i) \tag{5.4}$$

where K is a constant, since I is a constant.

However we know from biological observation that there is a maximum possible value of f, so that we can write $f \leqslant F$. A suitable approximation[2] to the value of f is therefore given by:

$$f = F\left[1-\exp\left\{-\frac{K(S-i)}{F}\right\}\right] \tag{5.5}$$

Hence $\qquad E = IF\left[1-\exp\left\{-\frac{K(S-i)}{F}\right\}\right] \tag{5.6}$

Now assume that at the end of a fibre, the stimulus conveyed to another neuron is given by:

$$S_2 = K_2 E_1 - T_k \frac{dS_2}{dt} \qquad (5.7)$$

where K_2 and T_k are constants. This gives:

$$S_2 = K_2 E_1 \left[1 - \exp \left\{ -\frac{(t-t_p)}{T_k} \right\} \right] \qquad (5.8)$$

on the assumptions that E_1 is constant and that $S_2 = 0$ when $t = t_p$. The excitation takes a time t_p to travel along the fibre. The first fibre excites the second neuron when $S_2 \geqslant i_2$. This occurs when:

$$\exp \left(\frac{t-t_p}{T_k} \right) = \frac{K_2 E_1}{K_2 E_1 - i_2} \qquad (5.9)$$

Hence it follows that:

$$t = t_p + T_k \ln K_2 K(S-i_1) - T_k \ln (K_2 K(S-i_1) - i_2) \qquad (5.10)$$

This expression gives the time at which the second neuron is excited It should be noted that the delay is a function of S.

5.5 SIMULATION OF NEURAL PROPAGATION

Many attempts to simulate neural transmission by use of electrical analogues have been made. Lillie[3] used a model made of iron wire immersed in nitric acid. Walter[4], who has himself constructed analogues using neon tubes, has criticised the Lillie model on the grounds that the nature of the insulating film in the iron-wire model is almost as mysterious as is that of natural nerve fibre. Walter used a cross-coupled arrangement of neon tubes which gave a visual demonstration of the neural type of propagation. Burns[6] used thyratron valves in a model neuron. Freygang[5] suggested the use of a resistance-capacitance transmission line with voltage pulse regenerators situated periodically along the line. Crane[7] considered various forms which artificial nerve fibres can take in practice. Nagumo *et al.*[8] and Yoshizawa *et al.*[9] have used the properties of tunnel diodes to provide the necessary pulse regeneration in artificial nerve fibres, while Cote[10] and Rosengreen[11] have used four-layer semiconductor devices.

There has thus been much work on the simulation of nervous transmission of information. There has not been the same emphasis on the use of closed neural loops for temporary information storage, though it seems that such a mechanism is almost certainly used in biological systems.

5.6 CLOSED NEURAL LOOPS

It has often been suggested that some memory storage in neural systems uses the properties of closed neural loops.[12] While it is most unlikely that permanent memory takes this form, judging from the non permanent results of such occurrences as concussion, it is quite possible that temporary information storage takes place in recirculating neural loops. A typical loop is illustrated in Figure 5.3

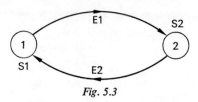

Fig. 5.3

A neuron having an excitation E_1 excites another neuron with excitation S_2. On the previously adopted assumption, we can write:

$$S_2 = K_2 E_1 - T_k \frac{dS_2}{dt} \qquad (5.11)$$

Now if a further fibre carries excitation from the second neuron back to the first, then we can write:

$$S_1 = K_1 E_2 - T_k \frac{dS_1}{dt} \qquad (5.12)$$

Substituting the earlier approximate forms for E_1 and E_2 we obtain:

$$S_2 = K_2 \, IF \left[1 - \exp\left\{ -\frac{K(S_1 - i_1)}{F} \right\} \right] - T_k \frac{dS_2}{dt} \qquad (5.13)$$

and:

$$S_1 = K_1 IF \left[1 - \exp\left\{ -\frac{K(S_2 - i_2)}{R} \right\} \right] - T_k \frac{dS_1}{dt} \qquad (5.14)$$

Now it is of interest to consider the conditions for unchanging S_2 and for unchanging S_1. The first is:

$$S_2 = K_2 IF \left[1 - \exp\left\{ \frac{K(S_1 - i_1)}{R} \right\} \right] \qquad (5.15)$$

This equation defines a curve on the S_2, S_1 plane. A similar curve is defined by the other condition:

$$S_1 = K_1 IF \left[1 - \exp\left\{ -\frac{K(S_2 - i_2)}{R} \right\} \right] \qquad (5.16)$$

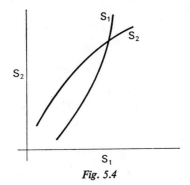

Fig. 5.4

If the two curves in the S_2, S_1 plane intersect, then a stable operating condition exists in which an impulse can continue to circulate around the neural loop once it is started. It is important to note that the actual exponential forms assumed are not essential for the results obtained to be true. It is merely essential that the actual algebraic forms make intersection possible, so that a stable solution, involving the storage of information, exists. The situation is illustrated in Figure 5.4

5.7 ELECTRONIC RECIRCULATING STORAGE

Recirculating neural loops make possible at least temporary storage of information. The present aim is to produce some of the characteristics of biological systems electronically. Information storage using recirculating loops is not unknown in electronic systems, and it is therefore of interest to study some of the characteristics of such systems.

Consider a positive feedback system having an input signal V_1, a forward transfer function $A \exp(-sT)$, an output signal V_0, and a positive feedback function B from output to input. We can write:

$$V_0 = (V_1 + BV_0)A \exp(-sT) \tag{5.17}$$

whence:

$$\frac{V_0}{V_1} = \frac{A \exp(-sT)}{1 - AB \exp(-sT)} \tag{5.18}$$

so that:

$$\frac{V_0}{V_1} = A \exp(-sT) \sum_{n=0}^{n=\infty} A^n B^n \exp(-nsT) \tag{5.19}$$

Practical systems have a finite bandwidth, so we can take the upper limit of summation as $n = N-1$:

$$\frac{V_0}{V_1} = A \exp(-sT) \sum_{n=0}^{n=N-1} A^n B^n \exp(-nsT) \qquad (5.20)$$

Expansion and subsequent contraction of this series of limited bandwidth gives:

$$\frac{V_0}{V_1} = A \exp(-sT) \left[\frac{1 - \{AB \exp(-sT)\}^N}{1 - AB \exp(-sT)} \right] \qquad (5.21)$$

$$= \frac{A \exp(-sT) - A^{(1+N)} B^N \exp\{-sT(1+N)\}}{1 - AB \exp(-sT)} \qquad (5.22)$$

From this it can be shown by a tedious though not difficult derivation that the real frequency response is given by:

$$\left| \frac{V_0}{V_1} \right| = \left(\frac{1 + A^{2(1+N)} B^{2N} - 2A^{(1+N)} B^N \cos \omega NT}{1 + A^2 B^2 - 2AB \cos \omega T} \right)^{1/2} \qquad (5.23)$$

where $\omega = 2\pi \times$ frequency.

In the special case where $A = 1$ and $B = 1$, the relationship simplifies to:

$$\left| \frac{V_0}{V_1} \right| = \left| \frac{\sin \dfrac{\omega NT}{2}}{\sin \dfrac{\omega T}{2}} \right| \qquad (5.24)$$

The obvious difficulty with a recirculating scheme is that caused by unavoidable non linearities in the record-replay system. Since this system forms a closed loop around which information must circulate, any signal will be degraded each time that it traverses the closed loop system. If the overall signal gain around this loop is greater than unity, then the signal will increase in amplitude each time it traverses the closed loop. Eventually the signal becomes so large that saturation in the record-replay system causes severe degradation of the signal.

If, on the other hand, the overall signal gain around the closed loop system is less than unity, then the signal is reduced in amplitude each time that it traverses the loop. Such a feature is actually desirable, since it ensures that more recently recorded information has a larger amplitude than information recorded earlier. However, if a very rapid decay of recorded information is to be avoided, the loop gain must be only very slightly less than unity.

From the mathematical derivation given earlier it can be seen that the input-output response of a sinusoidal recirculating system is zero at some frequencies, so it is not at all constant with frequency. This fact introduces additional difficulties.

5.8 THE EFFECT OF NOISE

It is necessary to consider the effect of electrical noise in a recirculating system of the type discussed earlier. It has been seen that:

$$\frac{V_0}{V_1} = A \exp(-sT) \sum_{n=0}^{n=\infty} A^n B^n \exp(-nsT)$$

Now if V_1 is a Gaussian noise waveform, then the mathematical series for V_0 contains noise components consisting of the noise delayed by nT and multiplied in amplitude by $A^n B^n$ etc., for values of n from 0 to infinity. The Root Mean Square value is given by the square root of the sum of the squares of all of the components. It is of interest to consider the ratio:

$$\frac{\text{RMS output noise}}{\text{RMS input noise}} = (1 + A^2 B^2 + A^4 B^4 + \dots\dots)^{1/2}$$
$$= (1 - A^2 B^2)^{-1/2}$$

This ratio shows that if the loop gain AB approaches unity in value, then the RMS noise is increased excessively by the positive feedback. Since the loop gain is required to be only very slightly less than unity in such a recirculating linear system, the use of positive feedback in this manner is not a desirable way of remembering occurrences or of storing neural information. However, it is worth while at this point continuing the investigation a little way to embrace the use of pulse sequences in recirculating systems, since such an investigation can reveal any additional difficulties likely to be experienced.

5.9 RECIRCULATING PULSES

A general expression for the transfer function of a recirculating positive feedback system is given by:

$$\frac{V_0}{V_1} = A \exp(-sT) \sum_{n=0}^{n=\infty} A^n B^n \exp(-nsT) \qquad (5.25)$$

Now suppose that the signal pulse transmitted in this system has the Laplace transform H_1, then a signal pulse delayed by a time $n_1 t_1$ has the transform $H_1 \exp(-sn_1 t_1)$. A sequence of such pulses occurring at multiples of time t_1 has the transform:

$$S_1 = H_1[1 + \exp(-sn_1 t_1) + \exp(-sn_2 t_1) + \exp(-sn_3 t_1) \dots] \quad (5.26)$$

where $n_1, n_2, n_3 \dots$ are integrals.

In the special case where the pulses form an evenly spaced train, $n_1, n_2, n_3, \ldots = 1, 2, 3, \ldots (N-1)$

then
$$S_s = H_1 \frac{[1 - \exp(-sNt_1)]}{[1 - \exp(-st_1)]} \tag{5.27}$$

Now if we apply the sequence of pulses having the transform S_1 to the filter having the response V_0/V_1 given above, the transform of the output is:

$$S_0 = S_1 \times \frac{V_0}{V_1} \tag{5.28}$$

$$= H_1[1 + \exp(-sn_1t_1) + \exp(-sn_2t_1) + \exp(-sn_3t_1)\ldots]$$
$$\times A \exp(-sT)[1 + AB \exp(-sT) + A^2B^2 \exp(-2sT)\ldots] \tag{5.29}$$

We can match the delay T to the period t_1.
In the special case where $n_1 = 1$, $n_2 = 2$, $n_3 = 3$ etc., this gives:

$$S_0 = H_1 A\, [\exp(-sT) + (1 + AB) \exp(-2sT)$$
$$+ (1 + AB + A^2B^2 \exp(-3sT) + \ldots] \tag{5.30}$$

and in this special case, the inverse transform is:

$$V_0 = L^{-1}H_1 A \exp(-sT) + L^{-1}H_1 A (1 + AB) \exp(-2sT)$$
$$+ L^{-1}H_1 A (1 + AB + A^2B^2) \exp(-3sT) + \ldots \tag{5.31}$$

Thus in this special case the output is expressed as a train of pulses spaced at intervals of T.

It is of interest to note that in the special case where $AB = -1$ (i.e. negative feedback, unity loop gain):

$$V_0 = L^{-1}H_1 A \exp(-sT) + L^{-1}H_1 A \exp(-3sT)$$
$$+ L^{-1}H_1 A \exp(-5sT) + \ldots \tag{5.32}$$

Thus in this special case, every other pulse is cancelled out by the preceding pulse, i.e. such an arrangement would perform the function of pulse frequency halving.

We are interested in the case where the loop gain AB is positive. What is the condition for the pulses to continue at constant amplitude after an input pulse train has finished? We are particularly interested in the condition for a single pulse to be retained.

If we insert a single pulse having transform H_1, then the output transform is:

$$S_0 = H_1 A \exp(-sT) + H_1 A^2 B \exp(-2sT) + H_1 A^3 B^2 \exp(-3sT)\ldots$$

Now if we require the pulse to be maintained recirculating with unchanged amplitude, we must have: $1 = AB = A^2B^2 = A^3B^3 = \ldots$ This is fulfilled by the conditions $A = 1$ and $B = 1$. However, if $A > 1$ we simply have an amplification of the input pulse amplitude by a factor A.

If we make the loop gain AB slightly less than unity, then the stored pulses gradually decay exponentially, the Nth output pulse being $A^N B^N$ times the amplitude of the first output pulse. The decay time constant is determined by:

$$A^N B^N = 0{\cdot}368$$

whence
$$N = \frac{\log{(0{\cdot}368)}}{\log{(AB)}}$$

Alternatively, the required loop gain can be determined from:

$$AB = (0{\cdot}368)^{1/N}$$

A loop gain of $0{\cdot}99$ will cause the amplitude of the 100th recirculated pulse to be $0{\cdot}368$ of the amplitude of the first pulse.

Unfortunately a very close control of effective loop gain AB is required if the pulses retained in such a system are to decay only slowly. For example, if the value of loop gain AB is equal to $0{\cdot}9048$, then the tenth recirculated pulse will have decayed to $0{\cdot}368$ of the amplitude of the first recirculated pulse. In order to delay this decay so that the amplitude reduction would not occur until one thousand pulses have been recirculated, the loop gain would have to be closely controlled to a value of $0{\cdot}9988$.

In addition to this requirement for close control of loop gain, it has been shown earlier that noise would be troublesome in such a linear recirculating system. From both points of view, it is therefore not desirable to use a simple linear dynamic recirculating system for storage of neural information. However, if signal regeneration and reshaping are included, then some of the problems can be overcome and an amount of noise which is reasonably small compared with the required pulse signals is not difficult to eliminate.

There is an additional economic practical problem which must be considered from an engineering point of view. If such dynamic recirculation is to be used in order to simulate neural storage, it is undesirable to require that a separate recirculating loop should be required in order to store each separate item of information, since this would lead to excessively complex memory arrangements for storage of quite small amounts of information in the nervous system. One possible method of overcoming this difficulty is based on the exclusive-product property of prime numbers.

REFERENCES

1. YOUNG, J. F., *Cybernetics*, Iliffe (1969)
2. RASHEVSKY, N., *Mathematical Biophysics*, Chicago (1938)
3. LILLIE, R. S., 'The Passive Iron Wire Model', *Biol. Rev.*, **11**, 181 (1936)
4. WALTER, W. G., *The Living Brain*, Duckworth (1953)
5. FREYGANG, W. H., 'Some Functions of Nerve Cells in Terms of an Equivalent Network', *Proc. IRE*, **47**, 1862 (1959)
6. BURNS, B. D., 'The Mechanism of After-Bursts in Cerebral Cortex', *J. Physiol.*, **127**, 168 (1955)
7. CRANE, H. D., 'The Neuristor', *Proc. IRE*, **50**, 2048 (1962)
8. NAGUMO, J., *et al*, 'An Active Pulse Transmission Line Simulating Nerve Axon', *Proc. IRE*, **50**, 2061 (1962)
9. YOSHIZAWA, S., *et al*, 'An Active Pulse Transmission Line', *Electr. and Commun. in Japan*, **46**, 22 (1963)
10. COTE, A. J., 'A Neuristor Prototype', *Proc. IRE*, **49**, 1430 (1961)
11. ROSENGREEN, A., 'Experimental Neuristor', Electronics, **36**, 25 (1963)
12. VERZEANO, M., and NEGISHI, K., 'Neuronal Activity in Cortical and Thalamic Networks', *J. Gen. Physiol.*, **43**, 177 (1960)

6 | Animal Learning

6.1 APPLICATION OF A PULSE TRAIN

The form of the neural activity encountered in the animal is now to be considered. Here the activity can be said to take the form of trains of pulses rather than the single pulses considered previously in isolation.

Consider a short train of pulses expressed by:

$$S_s = H_1 \frac{[1-\exp(-sNt_1)]}{[1-\exp(-st_1)]}$$

where there are N pulses in the train, spaced by time t_1.

Now let this pulse train be applied to a recirculating positive feedback system in which:

$$\frac{V_0}{V_1} = A \exp(-sT) \sum_{n=0}^{n=\infty} A^n B^n \exp(-nsT)$$

The output of the system then appears as the sum of an infinite number of delayed pulse trains having amplitudes which decrease exponentially as the delay increases.

An exponential increase and decrease of amplitude is just the form required in any memory system which is to incorporate a forgetting feature.

6.2 EFFECT OF NOISE WITH PULSE TRAIN INPUT

It has been seen that the effect of noise in a recirculating system can be expressed as:

$$\frac{\text{RMS output noise}}{\text{RMS input noise}} = (1 - A^2 B^2)^{-\frac{1}{2}}$$

Now if an evenly spaced train of N input pulses, each having a peak amplitude V, is applied to the recirculating system, then the peak value of the Nth output pulse is given by the summation:

$$\sum_{n=0}^{n=N-1} A^n B^n \times V = V\left(\frac{1-A^N B^N}{1-AB}\right)$$

Consequently:

$$\frac{\text{Peak output pulse amplitude}}{\text{RMS output noise}} = \frac{V}{N} \times \frac{(1-A^N B^N)(1-A^2 B^2)^{\frac{1}{2}}}{(1-AB)}$$

where V is the peak input pulse amplitude, and N is the RMS value of the input noise. It follows that:

$$\frac{\text{peak O/P pulse amplitude}}{\text{peak I/P pulse amplitude}} \times \frac{\text{RMS input noise}}{\text{RMS output noise}}$$

$$= \frac{(1-A^N B^N)(1-A^2 B^2)^{\frac{1}{2}}}{(1-AB)}$$

$$= (1-A^N B^N)\left(\frac{1+AB}{1-AB}\right)^{\frac{1}{2}}$$

This quantity can be considered as a figure of merit for noise reduction with such a memory system. The square root part increases rapidly as the loop gain AB approaches unity, while the $(1-A^N B^N)$ part falls at the same time. There is therefore an optimum value of AB which gives the best noise reduction, the value depending on the number N of pulses in the pulse train.

6.3 NON-LINEARITY

It will be noticed that in the above derivations, no specific steps have been taken to introduce non linearity into the loop gain AB. Biological nervous transmission appears to include continuous pulse reshaping. Similar pulse reshaping processes would be very easy to introduce into electrical storage loops, for example by the addition of a single saturating-type of non linearity at one point in the loop.

However, such a storage loop could not possess the feature of slow decay of stored information which was required in the present investigation. In a saturating type loop, the gain around most of the loop would exceed unity, and the saturation non linearity would then ensure that the overall effective gain was unity. There is no known way in such a non linear loop of providing an overall effective gain very slightly less than unity in order to ensure the required slow decay of the stored information.

One possibility here is the progressive narrowing of stored pulses in the loop. This might be done for example by slightly delaying the leading edge of a pulse while not delaying the trailing edge. While this would ensure the slow decay of stored information, it would necessitate circuit complication. It was decided instead to limit the investigation at this stage to a consideration of linear loop gain.

6.4 THE SIGNIFICANCE OF PROBABILITY

It is of interest to attempt a consideration of the extent to which probability theory, and hence the information theory[1] derived from it, are applicable in cybernetic systems. As each event occurs in a cybernetic system, the very fact of the occurrence of that event in the particular circumstances of the moment has the effect of changing the probability of future occurrences both of that event and also of other events whenever those particular circumstances happen to re-appear.

Consequently, probabilities are not at all fixed in value in the cybernetic system. They are continuously changing as the system learns, and care must be taken if there is an attempt to apply the theories of classical probability to such a case.

This segment of the field is in need of a rigorous review by mathematicians, though it is hoped that this will be undertaken by those mathematicians who are capable of reconverting their conclusions into a plain language form. Although such reconversion activity might appear prosaic in the extreme to the pure mathematician, it is an essential if the mathematician is to make any impact in the everyday applied field. Despite the information explosion, if the mathematician will carry out this reconversion it might give the humble engineer some chance of deciding whether or not he should take the time required to master the particular mathematical symbolism used. A scientist who published only in the Cornish language could hardly make more than a limited impact.

6.5 CONDITIONED REFLEX ACTION

In the seventeenth century, Descartes[2] discussed the occurrence in animals of reflex activity. Early in the present century, Pavlov[3] investigated conditioning of reflex action in animals. In his classic series of experiments he showed that if a bell was sounded each time that food was presented to an animal, eventually the bell alone could cause salivation, even though the food was not then presented. It is possible to explain much animal learning action in terms of conditioning of reflexes.

In effect, one stimulus A is associated with another stimulus B repeatedly until eventually stimulus A can on its own produce the response normal to stimulus B. It is important to note that the resulting conditioned response is not infallible. It appears rather that the probability of producing response B by stimulus A is increased by the repetition of the association. Since it is possible to explain a wide range of animal learning activity on this simple basis, it is of engineering interest to consider the feasibility of machines having similar capabilities.

Simple machines in which one or two inputs can be associated have been constructed and widely demonstrated.[4, 5, 7] However, it is not easy to extend such simple machines to handle a wide range of different inputs. It is most desirable that any such machine can be fairly easily extended, once the basic principles are clarified.

The means adopted for memory in some simple machines have produced traces which were transitory in the extreme. Examples are the storage of voltage on capacitors and decaying oscillation in electronic circuits. Such methods are not adequate if a thorough investigation of an extended machine is envisaged. Some of the methods of information storage which are used in digital computers are much more permanent,[8] but they are too inflexible for initial use in such research. They are, however, extremely valuable for later aspects of the research since it is possible to simulate a cybernetic machine with a general-purpose digital computer once the basic principles have been determined, and the practicability of the proposed approach for use in a compact form has been established. Some work on robots has unfortunately relied on the use of large digital computers from the initial stages, and it has been necessary for the mobile robot to be coupled to a large computer via flexible cables. Such an approach can hardly be expected to lead to a good engineering solution.

The means adopted for information storage should preferably give a permanent form of storage regardless of temporary failure of the power supply. The storage form should give non-destructive read-out, i.e. use of the stored information should not cause its destruction. The storage of new information should not affect previously stored information. However, there should be provision for the inhibition of older stored conditioned reflexes. The provision of some form of slow forgetting mechanism at a later stage must be kept in mind, so that the methods adopted in the initial design do not prevent the later addition of the forgetting feature.

It has been suggested by Hilgendorf[17] that the response time of the human to stimulation is proportional to the logarithm of the number of equiprobable alternative actions which might have to be taken.

A relationship such as this seems to apply up to at least 1000 different alternative possible actions. It is quite possible that such a limitation can be avoided in the robot.

The overall effect of a machine based on the requirements above should be probabilistic. It is not required that, once stimulus signals S_a and S_b have coincided, stimulus S_a should always inevitably produce effect e_b corresponding to stimulus S_b. Rather it is required that the probability of production of effect e_b by stimulus S_a should increase with the past frequency of occurrence of the coincidence (S_a, S_b).

There are thus three requirements for a store which can be used to display Pavlovian conditioning:

(1) Small size, preferably molecular
(2) Exclusive recording of coincidence
(3) Probabilistic recording of coincidence

An additional desirable factor would be that older recordings should decay slowly, so that they are of less importance than are more recent recordings. This forgetting process appears to be an important feature of animal activity.[9] While it is not essential to incorporate a forgetting process into initial work, the eventual need must be kept in mind. In effect, such a process helps to avoid overloading of the memory. In the animal case, it enables the animal to discard habits which are no longer of use in a changed environment or at a more advanced age. It is also desirable that an inhibitory process can be introduced if required.[6]

6.6 FORGETTING

It has been suggested more than once that there are two basic forms of human memory. One of these is said to be the long term or permanent memory. The other is considered to be a short term or temporary memory. There is some evidence for this type of action. For example, in cases of severe concussion, the most recent memories are lost permanently, and this is said sometimes to be due to the interruption of the temporary memory. It is also sometimes supposed that the contents of the temporary memory are selectively transferred to the permanent memory, and once in the permanent memory the stored facts can never be forgotten, though they can become subconscious and not too difficult to recall.

Unfortunately, it is not easy to provide concrete demonstrations of the process, partly because as in all psychological experimentation, it is almost impossible to remove all external influences. In such circumstances, the adoption of a simple model which exhibits an exponential decay is attractive.

It has been stated[10] that although it is possible for a human being deliberately to forget something in the short term memory, it is not possible voluntarily to forget anything once it is stored in the long term memory. It is perhaps necessary therefore to point out how obvious this fact is, since the very act of voluntarily attempting to forget must involve recall of the very subject that is to be forgotten. Voluntary forgetting of any given stored information is surely quite impossible by definition, in whatever part of the memory system the material is stored.

6.7 BASIC REQUIREMENTS

The initial basic requirements of an associatory learning machine are as follows:

(1) It must have some means of detecting coincidence between the occurrences of a number of input stimuli
(2) It must have some means of recording these coincidences
(3) It must have some means of making use of a recorded coincidence if any of the input stimuli occur in the future
(4) It should preferably operate on a probabilistic basis

There have recently been many different approaches to the construction of learning machines. The following are a few of the disadvantages noted by the writer in the course of reviewing such work.[11]

(1) Difficulty of extension. Whatever practical approach is adopted, it should not be limited to use with only a few inputs. Although it is difficult at present to envisage the extension of man-made devices to a biological level of complexity, the possibility of extension should be as unlimited as is practicable. This implies that sub-units should be simple, small and inexpensive.
(2) Error-free learning. Freedom from error has been widely used as a criterion of excellence in, for example, pattern-recognition machines.[12] However, such a criterion implies that each error must have a constant definition. This is not true of biological systems, which in general possess the property of adaptation to slow changes of the environment. The possession of the facility for forgetting is implied in this.
(3) Two-dimensional approach. It is a surprising fact that many workers have ignored the three-dimensional nature of the nervous system. This is particularly true of investigations of networks of artificial neurons, which have usually been limited to the two-dimensional approach.[13] (In some cases these networks have been simulated on a digital computer.[14])

In an associatory learning machine, if input signals S_a and S_b occur simultaneously, then a record $R(S_a, S_b)$ must be made. This record must be kept available so that if signal S_a occurs alone at a future time, then the effect e_b of signal S_b can be produced even though signal S_b is not actually occurring.

The recorded signal should be characteristic only of the associated input signals. For example, if the input signals are $S_a, S_b, S_c, S_d \ldots S_z$, then it must be true that the recorded signals:

$$R(S_a, \ldots S_b) \neq R(S_x, \ldots S_y)$$

where $S_x, \ldots S_y$ are any signals other than, $S_a, \ldots S_b$. It should be noted that this relationship must be fulfilled even if, to take a simple two-member example, $x = a$ but $y = b$. In this case again, we must have:

$$R(S_a, S_b) \neq R(S_a, S_y)$$

Thus any particular recorded coincidence $R(S_a, \ldots S_b)$ must be exclusive to a particular set of signals $S_a, \ldots S_b$ and must never correspond to any other set, including any set which differs from the original set by only one member.

It is an additional requirement that each and every subset coincidence should be separately detected and recorded, since each of these provides information which might be required by the machine at some future time. Indeed in the case of an organism, subset coincidence might be of vital future interest. Consequently it is necessary to arrange that:

$$
\begin{aligned}
R(S_a, S_b, S_c, S_d, \ldots S_z) = {}& R(S_a, S_b) + R(S_a, S_c) + \ldots \\
& \ldots + R(S_a, S_z) + R(S_b, S_c) + \\
& R(S_b, S_d) + \ldots R(S_b, S_z) + \\
& R(S_c, S_d) + \ldots R(S_c, S_z) + \\
& + \ldots + R(S_y, S_z)
\end{aligned}
$$

It is supposed that associations are recorded in pairs. This will include associations in threes, fours, etc., provided that there is a high probability that each and every pair association is recorded. One effect of this requirement is that the device is then capable of pattern completion or of operating on incomplete patterns of input stimulation.

An example will help to illustrate the requirements and difficulties. Suppose that there are four possible input signals S_a, S_b, S_c, S_d, and that the following associations occur:

$$R(S_a, S_b), \quad R(S_a, S_c), \quad R(S_a, S_c, S_d)$$

Now if all subset pairs are separately recorded then:

$$R(S_a, S_c, S_d) = R(S_a, S_c) + R(S_a, S_d) + R(S_c, S_d)$$

If this condition is met, then at some point in the future input signal S_a appearing without input signal S_c will be capable of producing association S_d, so that wrong information is stored. Signal S_a should not produce signal S_d unless signal S_c is also present. Thus it is necessary to ensure that

$$R(S_a, S_b, S_c, \ldots) \neq R(S_a, S_b) + R(S_a, S_c) + \ldots$$

It should be noted, however, that if this requirement is rigidly enforced then the machine will inherently only be capable of a minimal amount of pattern-completion.

It can be seen that there appear to be conflicting requirements:

(1) All subset pairs should be separately recorded, since every pair can provide useful information for pattern-completion.
(2) Subset pairs should not be separately recorded, since it is possible for a pair to provide incorrect information.

In the animal, it is possible that the conflict is resolved by three features:

(1) Probability
(2) Inhibition
(3) Forgetting

If the first of these features is incorporated, then the strength of the recorded information will depend on the frequency of past occurrence of the particular association. Consequently, information will be available for pattern completion. However, those associations which occur only coincidentally with other associations will be recorded less strongly than those associations which occur additionally in isolation.

The second feature would involve the addition of inhibition of associations which have not occurred in the past. While such a process possibly occurs to some extent biologically, it is not practicable to incorporate inhibition of every non-coincident association, since this would require excessive storage capacity.

The third feature is known to occur biologically. Its use would ensure that memory of those associations which occurred less frequently or only in coincidence with other associations would decay more rapidly than would the more frequent associations which also occurred in isolation.

At our present stage of knowledge about the human and animal learning process, the best method to resolve the conflict in an associatory learning machine is not known. It is therefore desirable that all three features should be capable where necessary of separate introduction, modification and elimination in such a machine. It will then be possible to carry out comparative tests on the use of the three features.

6.8 CONDITIONAL AND JOINT PROBABILITY

It was shown in the last section that a machine should be probabilistic, i.e. the probability of production of an effect e_b by a stimulus S_a should increase with the past frequency of occurrence of the coincidences of S_a with S_b.

Consider two events A and B which occur in the sequences shown in Figure 6.1, where each occurrence is marked by an asterisk.

A ✱✱✱✱✱✱

B ✱✱✱✱✱✱✱✱✱✱✱✱✱✱✱✱✱✱✱✱✱

Time ——————— t_1 ————————————————— t_2 ———

Fig. 6.1

If the conditional probabilities $P_A(B)$ and $P_B(A)$ are estimated from previous events, then at time t_1: $P_A(B) = 1$ and $P_B(A) = 1$, while at time t_2: $= P_A(B) = 6/21$ and $P_B(A) = 1$.

It is sometimes suggested that since at time t_2:

$$P_A(B) \neq P_B(A)$$

then those two probabilities should be recorded separately.[16] No doubt from a simple and purely mathematical point of view this is correct, but it ignores the physiological phenomenon of forgetting. If the point t_2 is far enough removed in time from point t_1, then the early association between A and B would be almost completely forgotten by any animal system.

We have no information on the exact law of forgetting, but it is tempting to postulate an exponential decay of memory traces.

Now at time t_1, $\qquad P_A(B) = P_B(A)$

but at time t_2, $\qquad P_A(B) < P_B(A)$

Thus any scheme involving the use of conditional probabilities must incorporate separate storage facilities for $P_A(B)$ and $P_B(A)$.

To obviate such separate storage facilities, and to give an improved economy of storage, it is suggested[15] that the memory system ought simply to store $P(A \text{ and } B)$. Then at time t_1 above, $P(A \text{ and } B) = 1$, but at time t_2 above, $P(A \text{ and } B) = 6/21$, i.e. $P(A \text{ and } B)$ has decayed because of non occurrence of the coincidence. Thus it is proposed that storage facilities are provided not for Conditional (or Unidirectional) Probabilities, but rather for Joint (or Bidirectional) Probabilities.

If there are N inputs $A, B, C, \ldots N$, then the Conditional or Unidirectional Probabilities are

$$P_A(B), P_A(C), P_A(D), \ldots P_A(N),$$

$$P_B(A), P_B(C), P_B(D), \ldots P_B(N),$$

$$P_C(A), \ldots \text{ etc.}$$

There are therefore $N(N-1)$ Unidirectional probabilities to be stored, if two-way associations are recorded.

However, the Bidirectional Probabilities are:

$$P(A \text{ and } B), P(A \text{ and } C), P(A \text{ and } D), \ldots P(A \text{ and } N),$$

$$P(B \text{ and } C), P(B \text{ and } D), \ldots P(B \text{ and } N),$$

$$P(C \text{ and } D), \ldots \text{ etc.}$$

There are therefore $\frac{1}{2}N(N-1)$ of these Bidirectional Probabilities for which storage provision must be made. The storage capacity ratio between Bidirectional and Unidirectional methods is therefore one-half, if two-way associations are recorded.

REFERENCES

1. YOUNG, J. F., *Information Theory*, Butterworths (1971)
2. DESCARTES, R., *A Discourse on Method*, Dent (1965)
3. PAVLOV, I. P., *Conditioned Reflexes*, Dover (1960)
4. WALTER, W. G., *The Living Brain*, Duckworth (1953)
5. ZEMANEK, H., KRETZ, H., and ANGYAN, A. J., *A Model for Neurophysiological Functions in Information Theory*, (ed. C. CHERRY) Butterworths (1961)
6. HUGGINS, P., 'Two Experimental Learning Machines', *JIEE*, **6**, 702 (1960)
7. ANGYAN, A. J., *Machina Reproducatrix, in Mechanics of Thought Processes*, 933 *HMSO* (1959)
8. STEINBUCH, K., and PISKE, U. A. W., 'Learning Machines and their Applications', *Trans. IEEE*, **EC12**, 846 (1963)
9. UNDERWOOD, B. J., 'Forgetting', *Sc. Amer.*, **210**, 91 (1964)
10. SUTHERLAND, N. S., 'Machines Like Men', *Science Journal*, **4**, 44 (1968)
11. YOUNG, J. F., *Cybernetics*, Iliffe (1969)
12. CHOW, C. K., 'An Optimum Character Recognition System Using Decision Functions', *Trans. IRE* **EC6**, 247 (1957)

13. MCCULLOCH, W. S., and PITTS, W. A., 'A Logical Calculus of the Ideas Immanent in Nervous Activity', *Bull. Math. Biophys.*, **5,** 115 (1943)
14. BEURLE, R. L., 'Properties of a Mass of Cells Capable of Regenerating Pulses', *Phil. Trans. Roy. Soc.* **240B,** 55 (1956)
15. YOUNG, J. F., 'Possibilities of a Sinusoidal Memory for an Extendable Cybernetic Machine', *J. IERE,* **39,** 9 (1970)
16. UTTLEY, A. M., 'The Transmission of information and the Effect of Local Feedback in Theoretical and Neural Systems', *Brain Research,* **2,** 21 (1966)
17. HILGENDORF, L., 'Information Input and Response Time', *Ergonomics,* **9,** 21 (1966)

7 | The Early Astra Machine

7.1 LEARNING AND FORGETTING CURVES

If it is assumed that the quantity to be stored is $P(A$ and $B)$, then it is possible to draw learning and forgetting curves for different circumstances by plotting the value of $P(A$ and $B)$ against time. This is done in Figure 7.1. It is assumed here that the stimulus B is repeated continuously while stimulus A appears as a short train of stimuli. The shape

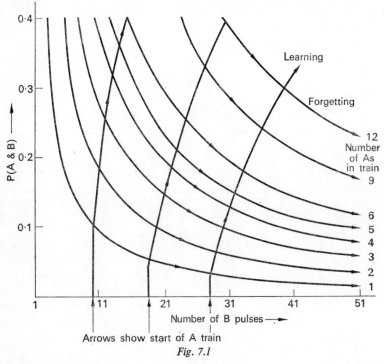

Fig. 7.1

of the resulting probability curve depends on the instant of occurrence and the length of pulse train A. Transfer from a learning curve to a forgetting curve takes place at the end of the A pulse train.

It should be noted that the relationship between the probabilities $P_A(B)$ and $P(A \text{ and } B)$ is given by:

$$P_A(B) = \frac{P(A \text{ and } B)}{P(A)}$$

Now the quantity $P(A)$ is always fractional or equal to unity, so it follows that:

$$P_A(B) \geq P(A \text{ and } B)$$

The curves of Figure 7.2 illustrate the relationships for a practical case.

It will be desirable to introduce such probability relationships into the operation of the machines envisaged here. While it is not absolutely

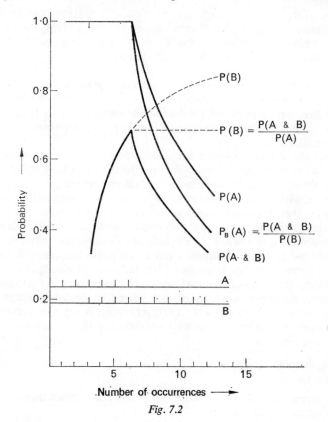

Fig. 7.2

necessary to incorporate these arrangements at the commencement of the work, the methods adopted must not prevent such incorporation at a later stage.

7.1 BASIC ASSOCIATION-LEARNING MACHINE

To provide an elementary demonstration of the principles of associatory learning of coincidental occurences between two inputs, a simple learning machine has been developed by Wood at Aston.

Externally, the demonstration machine consists of a box upon which is a diagrammatic representation of a nerve cell in the form of a triangle. Inputs are taken to two corners of this triangle from two sensing photocells. When either of the two photo-cells is shielded from the ambient light, a lamp lights at the corresponding corner of the triangular diagram.

One of the inputs is regarded as a reflex input and stimulation of the corresponding photo-cell always causes an output lamp to light at the remaining corner of the triangular nerve-cell diagram. However, stimulation of the other photo-cell alone never causes the lamp to light.

If now both photo-cells are stimulated, by shielding them from ambient light, simultaneously a number of times, eventually the second input becomes capable of producing the output and so causing the output lamp to light, even though the reflex input photo-cell is not then stimulated.

Thus this simple apparatus is capable of associating the coincidental stimulation of the two inputs and of producing a resulting conditioned reflex action. An additional feature is that the machine is arranged to forget slowly, so that if the reflex input alone is stimulated a number of times, then the conditioned action is lost or forgotten.

In this apparatus, each input photo-cell is arranged to control a pulse generator using a unijunction transistor. Continuous stimulation of the photo-cell input produces a pulse repetition frequency from the pulse generator which is at first high but then gradually falls, thus simulating the action of animal nerve cells when they are stimulated.

The resulting pulses are taken to a pulse-frequency-to-voltage convertor, which in turn controls a trigger circuit using complementary transistors. The output of each trigger circuit is then connected to the main memory unit.

The memory unit combines three of the characteristics of natural nerves, namely:

(1) The gradual association of two independent reflex inputs which occur together in time

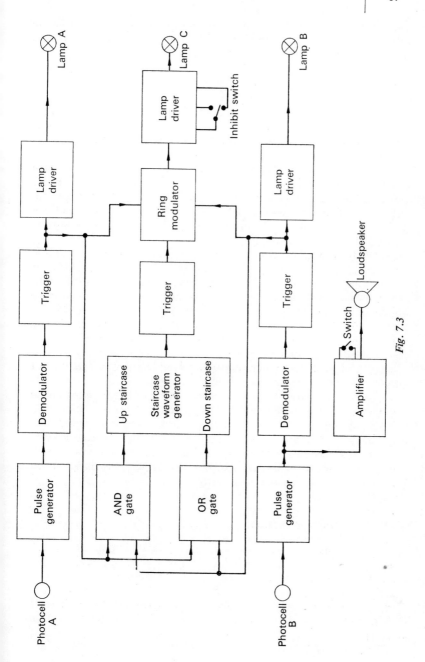

Fig. 7.3

(2) A tendency to forget associations between the two inputs if they only occur separately

(3) Inhibition. This uses an additional switch

Whenever the additional switch is closed, input *B* is arranged to inhibit the operation of the output lamp, even if input *A* is simultaneously operated.

Thus, with this unit it is possible to demonstrate some of the properties, both of animal nervous systems and of the ASTRA series of learning machines which have been investigated at Aston.

A block diagram of the arrangement adopted is given in Figure 7.3. Each photo-cell input drives a pulse generator. For demonstration purposes, one of the pulse generators is coupled to an amplifier which feeds a loudspeaker, so that the quasi-differentiated nature of the pulse repetition frequency can be heard.

Each of the pulse generators supplies a demodulator controlling a trigger circuit, which in turn controls the corresponding lamp driver circuit. If both inputs occur together, an AND gate is energised, and this produces an UP step to a staircase waveform generator. Thus each time that two inputs are simultaneously stimulated, the output of the staircase generator increases by one step.

If on the other hand either of the two inputs occur alone, then the DOWN input to the staircase generator is energised via an OR gate. This input is over-ridden by the AND input whenever both the two photo-cells are stimulated simultaneously. The staircase generator makes use of diode-pump circuitry followed by a field-effect transistor as a high-input-impedance amplifier. Another field-effect transistor is used as a discharge device to produce a stepped decay of the memory in the event of non-associatory occurrence.

The output from the staircase generator is taken to a trigger circuit, which gives an output only when the output of the staircase generator is above a certain level. A ring modulator integrated circuit is then used to ensure that lamp *C* can light whenever *A* is dark, or when *B* is dark and the trigger gives output.

7.3 SINUSOIDAL RECORDING

In an early attempt to produce an associatory learning machine, use was made of the properties of non-linear electrical circuits. For example, if two sinusoidal voltages having different angular frequencies are added together and applied to a squaring element such as a Hall crystal, then the lowest frequency output term can be separated out by filtering. In some cases, a single sideband form of modulator can be used.

The basis of a possible association-recording machine[1,2] based on

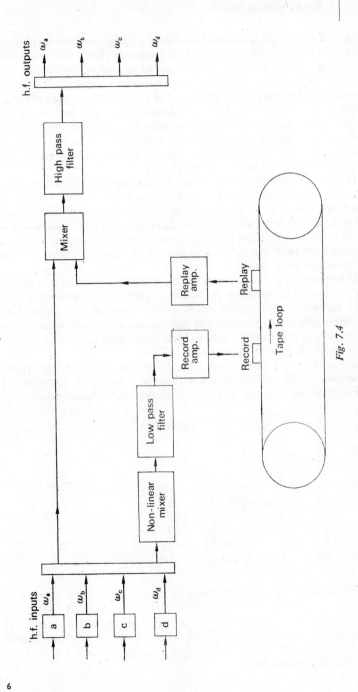

Fig. 7.4

the use of this single sideband modulator principle is shown in Figure 7.4. If, for example, oscillators a and b are energised simultaneously, producing signals at angular frequencies of ω_a and ω_b, then a signal of frequency $\omega_a - \omega_b$ is recorded on the magnetic tape loop. The signal $\omega_a - \omega_b$ can then be picked up from the tape via the replay arrangements at any time in the future to indicate that the two oscillators a and b have been simultaneously energised at some time in the past.

Before considering further how the recorded information might be used, it will be as well to consider obvious difficulties with the system described. There are two main problems:

(1) The recorded information can be ambiguous if the frequencies $\omega_a \ldots \omega_z$ are not carefully chosen. For example, if $\omega_c - \omega_b = \omega_y - \omega_x$, then there is no way of distinguishing between recorded signals indicating an association of c with b and those indicating an association of x with y. In order to avoid such ambiguity, a careful choice of oscillator frequencies is necessary, and this choice is not easy if a large number of inputs has to be handled.

(2) In the system as shown in the diagram, it is necessary to record newly-acquired information on to the magnetic medium directly over older recorded information, without first erasing the latter. This procedure introduces problems of partial erasure of older information and of loss of information due to tape saturation, and it is therefore not a desirable mode of operation.

In order to avoid the first difficulty, it is necessary to construct tables of numbers having exclusive differences (or possibly exclusive sums). To illustrate the problem, a simple difference table is given below.

f				Differences				
10								
11	1							
13	2	3						
17	4	6	7					
22	5	9	11	12				
30	8	13	17	19	20			
40	10	18	23	27	29	30		
54	14	24	32	37	41	43	44	
69	15	29						

The table has been constructed by inserting at the beginning of each line of differences the first difference integer which has not previously been used in the table. Eventually one encounters a number which has previously appeared and which is not therefore available. The final entry (29) in the above table is such a case, 29 having been used two lines previously.

In the above example, there are only eight integral values of f which can be used from the 44 equally spaced frequency channels nominally available. There are different ways of constructing such tables. For example, the second line of differences could have started with 3 instead of 2, giving:

f			*Differences*				
10							
11	1						
14	3	4					
19	5	8	9				
25	6	11	14	15			
32	7	13	18	21	22		
42	10	17	23	28	31	32	
44	2	12	19	25	30	33	34

Here the difference 2 has been introduced near to the end of the table. Eight channels are now usuable from only 34 instead of the 44 channels required by the previous table.

It is of interest to consider the effective channel utilisation in the case considered. The utilisation can be defined as:

$$\text{Channel Utilisation} = \frac{\text{number of usable channels}}{\text{number of available channels}}$$

Then for the first case considered above:

No. of Channels	1	3	7	12	20	30	44
Usable Channels	1	3	6	10	15	21	28
Utilisation %	100	100	86	83	75	70	63%

while for the second case above:

No. of Channels	1	4	9	15	22	32	34
Usable Channels	1	3	6	10	15	21	28
Utilisation %	100	75	66	66	68	66	82%

Consider yet another possible difference table:

2					
3	5				
4	7	9			
6	10	13	15		
8	14	18	21	23	
11	19	25	29	32	34

For this case:

No. of Channels	2	5	9	15	23	34
Usable Channels	1	3	6	10	15	21
Utilisation %	50	60	66	66	65	39%

6*

It is difficult to increase the number of usuable channels with the scheme discussed above, and it would be desirable to limit the rapid increase of values in the first column of the difference tables given in order to equalise the channel spacing as much as possible.

If the original frequencies could be made equal in value to the logarithms of prime numbers, then they would always have exclusive sums. Unfortunately such frequency values would be non-integral. In addition, the channel spacing would decrease as the numbers increased. These facts make the log(prime) approach of little value, even though published tables of such numbers[3] exist.

The absolute values of the frequencies f are of course of little importance, since the table of differences is the real basis of construction. In order to use other frequencies, the whole table can be multiplied by a constant, or a constant can be added to the frequency column.

7.4 CONTINUOUS RE-RECORDING

The recording of newly-acquired information over previously-recorded information introduces difficulties as mentioned earlier. In order to avoid such problems, the more complex arrangement shown in Figure 7.5 was considered and tried.

Here, the information recorded on the tape is picked up by a replay head. In addition to being taken to the output for external use, the replayed information is added linearly to new inputs and the sum is

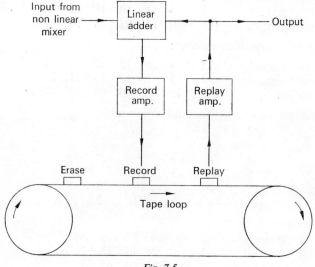

Fig. 7.5

recorded. An erase head ensures that the tape is magnetically clean before it reaches the recording head. With this system, the entire information about the past action of the machine is stored on the short length of tape between the record and replay heads. Such an arrangement can be thought of as being analogous to the neural recirculating loops believed to form part of the short-term memory system in animals.

7.5 SEPARATION OF INPUT FORMS

In the previous work, it has been assumed that all inputs to the system must be treated identically, and that it must be possible to associate any of the inputs with any other input. While such an approach gives a desirable generality, consideration of the animal case shows that such a generality might be quite unnecessary.

In the animal, it appears that there are various reflex actions which are built-in and almost unalterable, though effects such as atrophy due to lack of use are certainly possible. There are other inputs from the nerve sensors which are not directly associated with particular muscles at all. These nerve inputs can, however, become associated with the activity of particular reflex inputs by association.

If this form of associatory activity is applied to an artificial learning device, then the device should have two forms of input. These are:

(1) An input from a nerve sensor which is always and unalterably associated with the operation of a particular muscle. If the nerve is stimulated, then activity of the corresponding muscle tends always to follow. It might be necessary, however for the activity of several such nerve cells to coincide before muscle activity is stimulated.

(2) Other inputs from nerve sensors which are not directly associated with the operation of a particular muscle. If such a nerve is stimulated a number of times simultaneously, or almost simultaneously, with a nerve of the former type, then eventually the operation of the two nerves becomes associated, and the second sensor becomes capable of operation of the muscle directly, even in the absence of stimulation of the former reflex type.

If the operation of the nervous system is considered in this way, then it becomes useful to construct or to visualise a matrix of associations, with columns corresponding to various reflex or muscle activity, and the rows corresponding to the activation of the various nerve cells.

This approach has formed the basis for the work described earlier on the Lernmatrix. The disadvantage of the approach is that it would be very difficult to incorporate various natural phenomena into the rather inflexible magnetic core type of memory.

As applied to the magnetic recording form of memory device discussed here, the separation of the inputs into two different forms has the advantage that it is possible then to make use of more of the available storage space on the magnetic medium.

To illustrate this fact, consider a learning machine having nine reflex inputs at frequencies of 1000 Hz, 2000 Hz, ... 9000 Hz. If this machine also has nine nerve inputs at frequencies of 100 Hz, 200 Hz, ... 900 Hz, then a signal recorded on the magnetic medium at a frequency of say 3700 Hz is quite exclusive to one association. Consequently with a channel spacing of 100 Hz and in a bandwidth of 10 000 Hz, nine nerve and nine muscle or reflex inputs can be handled.

7.6 PRACTICAL ATTEMPTS WITH SINUSOIDAL RE-RECORDING

Two different forms of commercial magnetic recorder have been used in preliminary practical investigations of the continuous re-recording method for cybernetic memory. One form is the magnetic disc recorder, originally used as an early portable dictating machine.

It is not difficult to fit an extra recording head to one of these machines, together with the necessary additional electronic amplification. Such early machines had limitations in that the driving motor was clockwork, and the electronic amplifiers were battery operated. Nevertheless, with such machines it was possible to obtain preliminary experience of the difficulties encountered with the continuous re-recording of sinusoidal signals.

Additional work was carried out using commercial magnetic recording equipment. With such equipment, operated from an A.C. supply, the severe problems which can be caused by interference from external fields is encountered. Even small amounts of interference can be greatly enhanced in such a linear recirculating scheme.

It proves to be impractical simply to recirculate information in a sinusoidal form using magnetic recording, since the unavoidable distortion is cumulative. There is, however, some possibility of using such a method with the additional incorporation of re-shaping by the addition into the loop of some form of filtering. Such filters would also help to reduce the effects, again cumulative, of stray induced voltages. Some fast A.G.C. is also necessary.

REFERENCES

1. YOUNG, J. F., *Cybernetics*, Iliffe (1969)
2. YOUNG, J. F., 'Possibilities of a Sinusoidal Memory for an Extendable Cybernetic Machine', *JIERE*, **39**, 9 (1970)
3. CARMICHAEL, R. D., and SMITH, E. R., *Mathematical Tables and Formulae*, Dover (1962)

8 | Rectangular Waves

8.1 POSSIBLE USE OF CLIPPED SINE WAVES

The difficulties encountered with sinusoidal cybernetic memory systems are partly those of low distortion and of gain control. If rectangular, rather than sinusoidal waves were used in a recirculating loop information storage system, then it would be possible to have the gain around most of the loop in excess of unity. Reshaping of the stored waveform to the standard height and waveshape could then take place at a single point in the storage loop. It should perhaps be mentioned that biological storage and transmission systems make use of continuous reshaping of information during transmission,[1] rather than of reshaping at a single point.

In a system including reshaping at a single point in the recirculating loop, it would not matter at all if the storage loop had such a frequency response that the harmonic content of the stored rectangular wave was almost completely removed, leaving only the fundamental sine wave. Such a sine wave could then be clipped in order to reproduce the original rectangular wave. This clipping could be done by the use of various non-linear circuit elements, for example by use of a Zener diode.[2]

If both peaks are clipped from a sine wave, the Fourier expansion of the resulting wave approaches that for a rectangular wave as the severity of the clipping is increased. The writer has in the past adopted this form of peak clipping as a frequency-insensitive amplitude control in an oscillator giving a sinusoidal output at very low frequencies. It is of interest to note that at least one of the harmonics contained in a clipped sine wave can have zero amplitude, and this fact can be used for a sensitive control of the clipping level.

The method of magnetic recording of low-frequency width-modulated pulses for cybernetic purposes was successfully investigated at Aston in 1966 by Roberts and Coleman, who produced simplified equipment making use of low-cost tape recording equipment and transistorised circuitry. This work revealed some of the difficulties likely to be encountered with such a system, such as frequency and linearity limitations and anomalous behaviour with variations of pulse amplitude. It also led to possible circuitry simplifications and to investigations of automatic erasure when re-recording under saturation conditions.

In the association-machine, rectangular waves are added together in such a way that width-modulated pulses are produced.

8.2 LINEAR ADDITION OF RECTANGULAR WAVES

If two rectangular waves having equal amplitudes, but different repetition frequencies are added together linearly, then the resultant contains three levels as shown for example in Figure 8.1. Since the linear sum is being taken, the absolute level of the waveform is unimportant. However, this level has an effect if there is any non-linearity in the addition process.

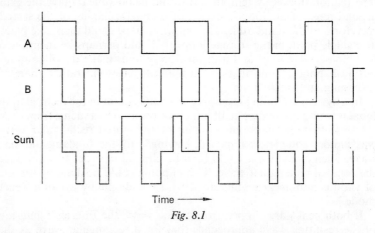

Time ⟶

Fig. 8.1

A further point of interest is that if the repetition periods are prime numbers, then the repetition period of the sum waveform is equal to the product of the repetition periods of the two constituent rectangular waveforms. Thus in the example, the repetition period of the first wave form is 5 units, the repetition period of the second waveform is 3 units, and the repetition period of the sum waveform is $5 \times 3 = 15$ units.

The linear sum of n rectangular waves of equal amplitudes but differing frequencies contains $(n+1)$ levels of amplitude. In Figure 8.1 the value of n is only equal to 2. However, the waveform of a linear sum wave rapidly becomes more and more complex as the number of components increases. Such a wave would not be suitable for re-shaping by use of simple amplitude clipping arrangements, and so this method of linear addition is not suitable on this count.

The outstanding reason why simple linear addition of rectangular wave signals cannot be considered is that the maximum overall amplitude which can occur is equal to n units if a number n of rectangular waveforms, each of unit amplitude, is added together linearly. This linear addition would lead to saturation in any practical recording medium. Such an effect would cause recorded information to be lost without hope of recovery. Thus although reshaping of summated rectangular waves is not impossible, this will not prevent loss of information if simple linear addition is used.

8.3 LOGICAL OPERATION ON RECTANGULAR WAVES

It has been seen that the simple arithmetic summation of a number of rectangular waves produces a resultant output wave which has a number of different amplitude levels and which is therefore not very suitable for re-shaping by use of non-linearities. It is consequently of interest to consider as an alternative the combination of rectangular waveforms by use of methods which are inherently incapable of producing more than two discrete output signal amplitude levels. One possible method is by generation of the logical product of rectangular waves, for example by use of logical gate circuits.

Consider two unidirectional rectangular waves v_1 and v_2, having identical amplitudes V but differing angular repetition frequencies ω_1 and ω_2. Now if these two waves are applied to the inputs of a two-way logical AND gate, then the output of the gate is given by the following table:

v_1	v_2	O/P
O	O	O
O	V	O
V	O	O
V	V	V

This table should be compared with a table of instantaneous products of v_1 and v_2. The products can each have one of only two different values, O and V^2.

v_1	v_2	Product
O	O	O
O	V	O
V	O	O
V	V	V^2

From this it is seen that the logical AND gate gives the required output modified only by a scale factor.

If v_1 and v_2 are rectangular waves then the product $v_1 v_2$ is given by the expansion:

$$V^2/4 + V^2/\pi[\sin \omega_1 t + (1/3) \sin 3\omega_1 t + (1/5) \sin 5\omega_1 t + \ldots$$
$$+ \sin \omega_2 t + (1/3) \sin 3\omega_2 t + (1/5) \sin 5\omega_2 t + \ldots]$$
$$+ 4V^2/\pi^2[\sin \omega_1 t \sin \omega_2 t + (1/3) \sin \omega_1 t \sin 3\omega_2 t$$
$$+ (1/5) \sin \omega_1 t \sin 5\omega_2 t + \ldots$$
$$+ (1/3) \sin 3\omega_1 t \sin \omega_2 t + (1/9) \sin 3\omega_1 t \sin 3\omega_2 t$$
$$+ (1/15) \sin 3\omega_1 t \sin 5\omega_2 t + \ldots$$
$$+ (1/5) \sin 5\omega_1 t \sin \omega_2 t + (1/15) \sin 5\omega_1 t \sin 3\omega_2 t$$
$$+ (1/25) \sin 5\omega_1 t \sin 5\omega_2 t + \ldots + \ldots]$$

Here the first term is a constant. The second term is simply formed from the algebraic sum of the two original rectangular waves.

If the steady component was removed from the original rectangular waves so that:

$$v_1 = 2V/\pi[\sin \omega_1 t + (1/3) \sin 3\omega_1 t + (1/5) \sin 5\omega_1 t + \ldots]$$
$$v_2 = 2V/\pi[\sin \omega_2 t + (1/3) \sin 3\omega_2 t + (1/\omega_2 5) \sin 5\omega t + \ldots]$$

then the product wave would only contain the third set of terms in the expansion above, the first term and the second set being eliminated entirely.

Unfortunately, removal of the steady component of the original waves changes the possible instantaneous levels from V and O to $+V/2$ and $-V/2$. Consequently the table of instantaneous products becomes

v_1	v_2	*Product*
$+V/2$	$+V/2$	$+V^2/4$
$+V/2$	$-V/2$	$-V^2/4$
$-V/2$	$+V/2$	$-V^2/4$
$-V/2$	$-V/2$	$+V^2/4$

The action corresponding to this table can be obtained by use of an inverted exclusive-OR arrangement as shown for example in Figure 8.2 though this is not the only way to implement such a logical product table.[3]

The writer has used such an arrangement as a generator of triangularly pulse-width-modulated test signals for p.w.m. amplifier systems. A convenient graphical way of visualising the effects of input frequency changes was shown to be the use of a 'chess-board' representation

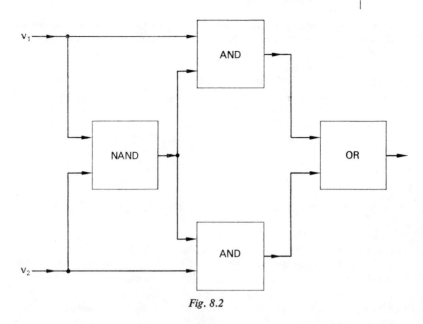

Fig. 8.2

of the two inputs. In this the two axes represent the rectangular wave inputs and shaded areas represent regions where both inputs are simultaneously positive. Various effects can then be shown.

8.4 USE OF A GATE AS A SELECTIVE FILTER

If rectangular waves are mixed to obtain the logical product as suggested earlier, then this logical product waveform contains the required past-association information for application to the memory. If this information is stored, then provision must be made for its utilisation at a future time.

If the occurrences of inputs *A* and *B* have coincided in the past, then excitation of the rectangular wave generators having frequencies ω_A and ω_B has coincided in the past. These rectangular waves have been mixed and the results have been stored. The stored information takes the form of a triangularly pulse-width-modulated wave.[4] Now the problem must be considered of how this stored information is to be used in the future.

If one of the inputs, say *A*, occurs alone in the future, then it must be possible to make use of this input *A*, together with the information stored in the memory about the past association of input *A* with input *B*, to produce excitation of the output *b* which corresponds to input *B*. In this way the remembered past association of *A* and *B* can be used to cause excitation of a particular output *n*, not only by the occurrence of its corresponding input *B* but also by the occurrence of the associated input *A*.

It would be possible to use tuned circuits as selective output filters, together with some form of mixing device as envisaged in the earlier sinusoidal scheme. However, there would be several disadvantages in the use of such a method. The schemes discussed here are envisaged for eventual use with a very large number of inputs and outputs. The resulting large bank of filters would be bulky, since inductances would be required. The inductances would have to be shielded in order to prevent effects caused by extraneous fields. If a magnetic recorder was used as the memory device the speed would have to be closely controlled. Any change of inductance due to drift would introduce additional problems if a very large bank of filters was involved.

As an alternative to the use of tuned filters, logical selective gates can be used. As an example, a two-input AND gate with one input connected to a master frequency pulse supply will only give a large mean value of output if the other input is connected to a source producing pulses at the same frequency. Any difference between the two frequencies will cause beats to appear and there will be a reduction of the mean output from the gate. Thus such a gate can be used as a selective filter if one input is connected to a master pulse source.

8.5 RECTANGULAR WAVE ANALYSIS

Consider a recorded triangularly pulse-width-modulated wave as produced by a simple AND gate to be applied to one input terminal of a further logical AND gate. The other input terminal is connected to a test source producing a rectangular wave at a repetition frequency almost equal to that of one of the original constituent rectangular waves. Then the mean output of the AND gate varies slowly at the difference frequency between the recorded frequency and the newly-applied frequency.

The frequency of the rectangular wave from the test source can be made exactly equal to the frequency of one of the originally associated rectangular waves contained in the recorded triangularly pulse width modulated wave. The output of the gate is then reduced to zero provided that the test rectangular wave is exactly in antiphase to, as well as equal in frequency to, one of the original rectangular waves. An example of this action is shown in Figure 8.3. Here the original associated signals had repetition periods of five units and of three units respectively. The logical addition of these two waveforms produces the width modulated waveshape shown. The logical addition of

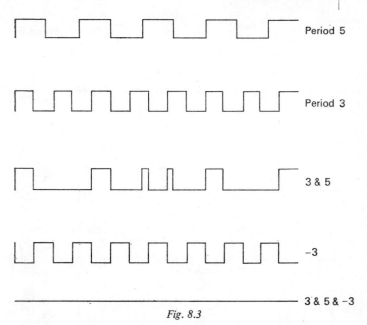

Period 5

Period 3

3 & 5

-3

3 & 5 & -3

Fig. 8.3

this logical sum waveform to the negative of the rectangular wave having a period of three units then gives a zero output from the AND gate as shown. Similarly, the application of the negative of the rectangular wave having a period of five units will give a zero output. On the other hand, the application of a rectangular wave with a period of for example four units gives an output as shown in Figure 8.4.

Detection of the null can be used in a very sensitive selective filter arrangement. In the present case, when a particular frequency is applied, such an arrangement can be used to detect the presence of a recorded association with that frequency. In logical terms, the process can be expressed as:

$$(A.B.C)\bar{B} = B.\bar{B} = 0$$

However, it is not sufficient simply to determine that there has been an unspecified association in the past. It must be possible to determine the actual frequency of the rectangular wave which has in the past been associated with the presently impressed wave.

Now a triangularly pulse-width-modulated wave can be formed by the logical addition of two rectangular waves neither of which has any steady content. It is convenient here to consider a simple specific example. In Figure 8.5 two waves having repetition periods of five

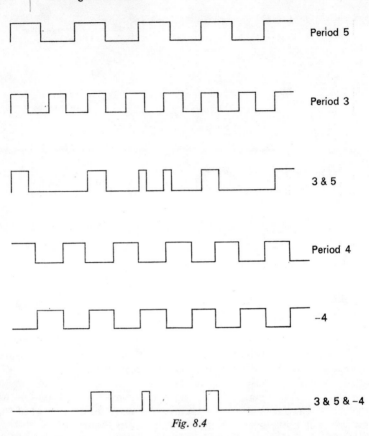

Fig. 8.4

units and three units respectively, and each having a mean value of zero, are logically added in an exclusive OR circuit to produce the wave shown. This wave is an elementary form of pulse-width-modulated wave. Now suppose that this wave is applied to one terminal of a further exclusive-OR circuit, while a zero-mean content rectangular wave of repetition period three units is applied to the other input terminal. The output of the exclusive-OR circuit is then the associated rectangular wave of five units period as shown in Figure 8.5. The logic statement of this approach is:

let $\qquad A.\bar{B}+\bar{A}.B = Z$

then $\qquad B.Z+\bar{B}.Z = B(A.B+\bar{A}.\bar{B})+\bar{B}(A.\bar{B}+\bar{A}.B)$

$$= A.B+A.\bar{B}$$

$$= A$$

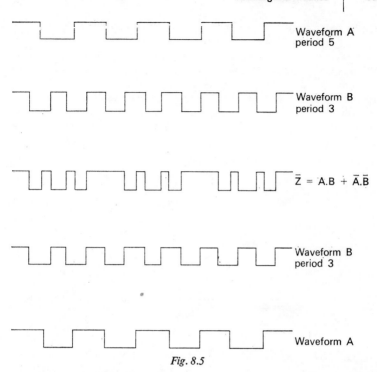

Fig. 8.5

It should be noticed, however, that the exclusion of unwanted output is not at all complete with this method. While the correct associated waveshape is always obtained when an associated signal is applied, non-associated signals are not prevented from producing an unwanted output. This output will not be a periodic rectangular wave such as those given by the correct associated signals, and it can therefore be eliminated by further filtering.

It is of interest to compare the mixing of rectangular waves as discussed here with the optical work which has been carried out on Moiré fringes and their applications.[5]

8.6 DEMODULATION WITH SYMMETRICAL RECTIFIER

In the course of work on the methods discussed here, it is necessary to investigate the form of the recorded width-modulated pulses. In the methods considered, the information about past associations is stored on the magnetic recorder in the form of pulses of variable widths. As has been seen, the association of two rectangular waves results in the production of a triangularly pulse-width-modulated wave. Demodulation of such waves is commonly achieved by the use of simple low-pass filters. While this is adequate for many audio applications, there is a severe loss of information at the higher frequencies, and for example a triangular wave is degraded in such a filter to become a waveform little different from a sine wave. It was felt that better methods should be available in the present research. Accordingly, the possibilities of the method of symmetrical rectification were investigated.

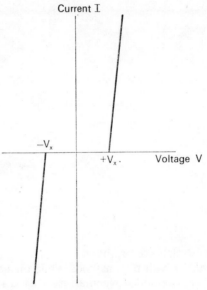

Fig. 8.6

The writer has shown elsewhere[6] that a device having a perfectly symmetrical though non-linear characteristic such as that of Figure 8.6 is suitable for use as a rectifier of pulse waveforms. If a waveform such as that of Figure 8.7 with an on-time of t_a and a repetition period of t_k

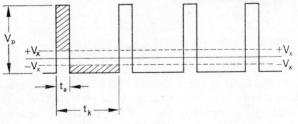

Fig. 8.7

and having no D.C. content, is applied to an ideal rectifier of this type, the mean value of the output of the rectifier is given by the linear relationship:

$$V_{mean} = V_x\left(1 - 2\frac{t_a}{t_k}\right)$$

It is assumed here that both the maximum positive and the maximum negative levels of the waveform exceed the clipping level V_x of the symmetrical rectifier. This assumption is fulfilled provided that the peak-to-peak height V_p of the rectangular waveform is:

$$V_p > \frac{V_x t_k}{t_a}$$

Within this limitation, the mean output of the symmetrical rectifier is proportional to the mark-to-period ratio of the applied rectangular wave. Thus the relationship is linear, passing through zero at the

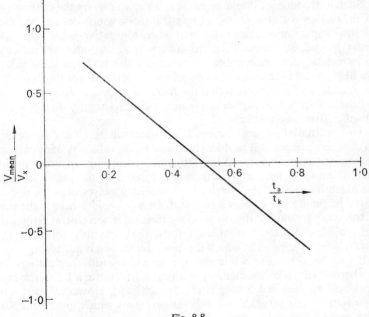

Fig. 8.8

point where $t_a/t_k = 0{\cdot}5$, as shown in Figure 8.8. Thus the symmetrical rectifier is an ideal device for use as a demodulator of pulse-width-modulated signals.

In the present investigation, the symmetrical rectifier is of use for the conversion of the triangularly pulse-width-modulated pulses into a triangular waveform. Such a converting device is required in the equipment considered here. The necessity for the incorporation of such a conversion is discussed in the next section.

8.7 DIFFICULTIES WITH PULSE-WIDTH-MODULATION

There are certain basic practical difficulties which would have to be overcome before pulse-width-modulation could be used in the memory circuits of an associating type of learning machine. It would be possible to regenerate and to recirculate the stored information, though some degredation must be expected due to shifts of the edges of the pulses during the regeneration process. Fortunately, both leading and trailing edges of the pulses should be shifted by the same amount in a purely linear system. However, this will not be true if the system has change-over characteristics which depend on the direction of change.

Such a dependence could be caused, for example, by the cutting-off of an emitter-follower using an *npn* transistor which occurs because of stray capacitance across the load when a negative-going edge appears. More fundamentally, carrier storage in semiconductors is likely to introduce such undesirable asymmetrical effects. Even small shifts are likely to be exaggerated in any scheme which features the dynamic recirculation of information in pulse form. It is noteworthy that biological systems which feature continuous pulse reshaping do not seem to suffer from such defects.

This recirculation degredation is an unfortunate effect. However, an even more important problem is caused by the difficulty of adding-in new information to a variable-width pulse recording. In order to do this, it would be necessary to modify the width of the pulses to give the algebraic sum of the width of the recorded pulses plus the width of the incoming pulses plus a constant. One possibility here is the use of the symmetrical rectifier to produce triangular waveforms from the pulse-width-modulated recorded information, possibly followed by filters, before the point at which the new information is added-in.

It can be seen that while the use of pulse-width-modulation in a cybernetic association-memory is a possibility, quite a lot of further work will be required before it can be achieved. However, work on such systems has revealed some of the problems which must be faced with more advanced systems of association-memory. As an example, it becomes clear from such work that it is desirable to derive all pulse signals used in the system from a master track recorded on the magnetic recording medium. Another example is the necessity for special provision in the electronic circuitry to cater for the join in the loop of magnetic tape or the start point on the magnetic drum. In such work it is now possible to make use of the advances which have been made in the magnetic recording methods for digital computers.

In the recording of pulse-width-modulated information, it is not necessary to record the actual pulse width-modulated wave on the magnetic medium. The change-over times of the pulses convey all of the information contained in a wave, since the amplitude of the wave is constant. In fact, if a pulse wave is applied direct to a magnetic recording head, the reproduce head merely gives a short differentiated pulse each time that the recorded pulse changes polarity. A bi-stable circuit can reconvert these pulses to a pulse-width-modulated form. However, the difficulties lead to an alternative, the direct use of the short pulse in the memory.

REFERENCES

1. NAGUMO, J., *et al*, 'An Active Pulse Transmission Line Simulating Nerve Axon', *Proc. IRE*, **50**, 2061 (1962)
2. YOUNG, J. F., A Simple Very-Low-Frequency Oscillator', *Electronic Engineering*, **31**, 218 (1959)
3. YOUNG, J. F., 'Variable-Polarity Logic', *Control*, **9**, 493 (1965)
4. YOUNG, J. F., 'The Generation of Triangularly Pulse-Width-Modulated Waves', *Electronic Engineering*, **38**, 787 (1966)
5. DAVIES, B. J., *et al.*, 'A High-Resolution Measuring System Using Coarse Optical Gratings', *Proc. IEE*, **107B**, 624 (1960)
6. YOUNG, J. F., 'Rectification Using Devices Having Symmetrical Characteristics', *Electronic Engineering*, **38**, 461 (1966)

9 | Recirculation

9.1 POSSIBILITY OF NON-DYNAMIC RECIRCULATION

Following the precedent set by the apparent method of operation of the short-term memory arrangements in biological systems, the memory systems discussed above have been based on the use of dynamic storage of information. Such an approach shows some promise for use in certain engineering systems. However, it can be seen that difficult problems remain to be solved in the practical development of such dynamic systems.

The problems are mainly those, such as noise augmentation, introduced by the dynamic nature of the storage arrangements. If dynamic storage is indeed used in biological information storage systems, it is clear that these problems can be overcome. However, this fact does not necessarily imply that the best engineering solution at the present time is the closest possible copy of the biological method.

It has been shown in the earlier work that a possible advantage of dynamic recirculation is the easy way in which the important forgetting or information-overload-avoiding process could be incorporated automatically. This again is an advantage if a direct simulation of biological processes is required. However there are other possible ways in which a forgetting process could be incorporated, and it might be better to consider the use of these alternative methods in engineering systems. If the alternative methods are adopted, then the absolute necessity for the use of dynamic storage methods no longer exists, and the use of non-dynamic methods becomes worthy of investigation. Such non-dynamic methods, together with forgetting arrangements, are required anyway for permanent cybernetic memory systems.

A dynamic memory arrangement loses its entire content of stored information in the event of even temporary failure, for example of the power supply circuits. While biological evidence apparently indicates that this phenomenon does occur, for example in the case of concussion, it is only the information in the short-term memory which is lost and long-term memories do not disappear permanently. Thus it is very unlikely that long-term memories are stored in dynamic form.

With a non-dynamic recirculation system such as that discussed, the information stored is determined entirely by the position on the magnetic medium at which a memory pulse is recorded. Consequently, any variation in speed of the mechanical drive arrangements of the magnetic recorder can have the effect of completely changing the apparent nature of the stored information. This could be a serious practical disadvantage of the system.

There are two possible solutions to this problem. First, the speed of rotation of the mechanical drive of the magnetic recorder could be rigidly controlled with reference to an extremely stable master frequency source. For example, the drive could take the form of a servo system in which the reference frequency was drived from a temperature-controlled quartz crystal oscillator of extreme stability. Such an arrangement would be quite complex.

Fortunately, there is a simpler possible alternative arrangement. In this method, all of the signals used in the overall system are derived from a single master source of clock pulses. The required master clock pulses are derived from a continuous train which is recorded on one master track of the recording medium. Signal pulses having the various required repetition periods can be derived from this master track by counting, using for example electronic counters. Coincidences between the signal pulses can then be recorded on to a separate memory track on the same recording medium as is used for the permanent master track. There is then no possibility of loss of synchronism between the source of master pulses and the source of memory signals, since both sources exist side-by-side on the same medium.

The two methods suggested here for overcoming the effects of variation of speed of the recording medium can be compared directly with the corresponding methods introduced by Williams and West[1] and by Booth[2] for use in the magnetic memories adopted in digital computers.

There is a number of possible methods which might be used for the non-dynamic storage of information. These can be divided into two general classes:

(1) Those static methods in which all stored information is immediately available. An example is the use of magnetic cores.

(2) Those methods in which any particular item of stored information is only available periodically. An example is the use of a magnetic tape or drum.

In biological memory systems, immediate access of information is found to be not essential. Consequently, it is possible to concentrate on the second class of non-dynamic information storage methods.

When the magnetic tape or drum method of non-dynamic

recirculation of stored information is used, the association signals are to be permanently recorded whenever an association occurs between inputs. The recording is then to be mechanically recirculated over and over again. This recorded association information can then be periodically extracted and used in the future if any of the previously-associated inputs re-occur. For example, the association signals can be permanently recorded in pulse form at definite points on a continuous loop of magnetic tape. The recorded signals can then be continuously recirculated past a replay head by driving the loop of tape at a constant speed. A magnetic recording drum could be used in the same way. It should be noted that the recorded information is retained in magnetic form even if the power supplies are removed and if the mechanical drive ceases.

9.2 PRIME PERIOD STORAGE PRINCIPLE

The basic idea behind the method of association memory storage using the properties of primes can be stated quite simply. The periods (rather than the frequencies as in earlier schemes) of the input signals are to be based on prime numbers. The repetition periods of input pulses are all to be different prime integral multiples of the period of a master clock pulse. Consider, for example, short pulses having a prime repetition period of 3 units of time, which occur during the same interval as other short pulses having a prime repetition period of 5 units of time. Assume that the two sets of pulses are applied to the two inputs of a logical AND gate. Then the output of the AND gate will consist of pulses of coincidence, having a period of 15 units of time. Such a signal is absolutely exclusive to the two prime repetition periods 3 and 5 and it cannot be produced by signals having any other prime repetition periods.

The method of use of this approach[3] can be described with reference to Figure 9.1. Here, pulses A, having a prime repetition period of three units of time are produced during the same interval as are pulses B, having a prime repetition period of five units of time. The two pulses

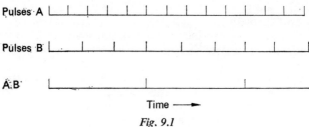

Pulses A

Pulses B

A.B

Time ⟶

Fig. 9.1

therefore coincide every fifteen units of time. Pulses having this repetition period can be recorded to indicate the past occurrence of coincidence.

If then in the future pulses A occur alone, they will coincide with the recorded information at every fifteenth interval, and this point in time also coincides with a B pulse. The coincidence of the new A pulses with the recorded $A.B$ pulses can therefore be used to gate pulses from the B source to an output actuator if required. There can be no confusion with such a system because a pulse recorded at a given product interval can correspond only to two prime input intervals. With this scheme, it is possible to interleave the storage so that a single storage medium can be used to store the associations between numbers of different prime input pulses. Such a feature leads to an economy of storage, an advantage shared by the earlier schemes using sinusoidal and rectangular wave signals.

In order to use this scheme, sources of the various pulses are required, and so are coincidence detectors. If the coincidence detectors take the form of AND gates, then a large number of gates is required. For example, with five different possible pulse inputs A, B, C, D, E, all having different prime repetition periods, it is necessary to have ten AND gates for $A.B$; $A.C$; $A.D$; $A.E$; $B.C$; $B.D$; $B.E$; $C.D$; $C.E$; $D.E$. Fortunately, matrix boards into which diodes can be plugged are now readily available.

9.3 BASIS OF THE SHORT-PULSE METHOD

A practical short pulse can be considered as the sum of a positive exponential rise and a delayed negative exponential rise. Thus the Laplace Transform for the short pulse

$$= \frac{1}{s} \times \frac{1}{1+sT} - \frac{1}{s} \times \frac{1}{1+sT} \times \exp(-s\tau) \qquad (9.1)$$

$$= \frac{1-\exp(-s\tau)}{s} \times \frac{1}{1+sT} \qquad (9.2)$$

where T is the rise time constant and τ is the time length of the pulse It has been assumed that the rise and fall time constants of the pulse are approximately equal in value.

In the present system, pulses like this are delayed by various times $N_1 t_a$, $N_2 t_a$, $N_3 t_a$, etc., where t_a is the master pulse repetition period and N_1, N_2, N_3, etc. are numbers of the form:

(Prime product)$\times$(some number X)

Hence the Laplace transform of the recorded waveform is:

$$\frac{1-\exp(-s\tau)}{s} \times \frac{1}{1+sT} [\exp(-N_1 t_a s) + \exp(-N_2 t_a s)$$
$$+ \exp(-N_3 t_a s) + \ldots] \qquad (9.3)$$

Now this recorded waveform is compared logically with inputs of the form:

$$\frac{1-\exp(-s\tau)}{s} \times \frac{1}{1+sT} \times \exp(-N_x t_a s) \qquad (9.4)$$

where N_x takes the form (Prime number)$\times$(some number Y)

If it ever occurs that:

$$L \exp(-N_x t_a s) = L[\exp(-N_1 t_a s) + \exp(-N_2 t_a s) + \ldots] \quad (9.5)$$

where
$$L = \frac{1-\exp(-s\tau)}{s} \times \frac{1}{1+sT} \qquad (9.6)$$

then an association corresponding to the present input is present on the recording and an output is required. The requirement is satisfied if ever

$$N_x t_a = N_y t_a \quad \text{where} \quad N_y \quad \text{is one of} \quad N_1, N_2, N_3, \text{etc.}$$

or
$$N_x = N_y$$

Now N_x and N_y are products of integers:

$N_x = $ (Prime number Q)$\times$(Some number Y)
$N_y = $ (Prime product RS)$\times$(Some number X)

The equality is therefore satisfied if $Q = R$ and $Y = SX$, or if $Q = S$ and $Y = RX$. Note must also be taken of the case $X = Q$ and $Y = RS$, since this places a limitation on the range of numbers which can be used in the system.

9.4 PULSE PRODUCT TRAINS

Consider an infinite series of pulses of unit height, each having a time duration of $2t_1$ seconds and a repetition period of T seconds, as illustrated in Figure 9.2.

Such a pulse train can be expressed as:

$$\theta(t) = \frac{2t_1}{T} + 2 \sum_{n=1}^{n=\infty} \frac{\sin 2\pi n t_1/T}{n\pi} \cos \frac{2\pi n t}{T} \qquad (9.7)$$

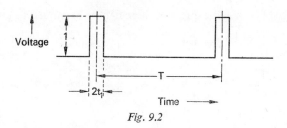

Fig. 9.2

However, if $t_1 \ll T$, then:

$$\sin 2\pi n t_1/T \rightarrow 2\pi n t_1/T$$

The amplitude of each harmonic then approaches $4t_1/T$.

For convenience, we can suppose that the pulse height is equal to $1/2t_1$, so that the amplitude of each component approaches $2/T$, and equation (9.7) becomes:

$$= \frac{1}{T} + \frac{2}{T}\cos 2\pi\frac{t}{T} + \frac{2}{T}\cos 4\pi\frac{t}{T} + \frac{2}{T}\cos 6\pi\frac{t}{T} + \ldots \quad (9.8)$$

Now consider two separate pulse trains having pulse repetition periods of U and V respectively. The first train can be expressed as:

$$\theta_1 = \frac{1}{U} + \frac{2}{U}\cos 2\pi\frac{t}{U} + \frac{2}{U}\cos 4\pi\frac{t}{U} + \frac{2}{U}\cos 6\pi\frac{t}{U} + \ldots \quad (9.9)$$

while the second train can be expressed as:

$$\theta_2 = \frac{1}{V} + \frac{2}{V}\cos 2\pi\frac{t}{V} + \frac{2}{V}\cos 4\pi\frac{t}{V} + \frac{2}{V}\cos 6\pi\frac{t}{V} + \ldots \quad (9.10)$$

The product of these two pulse trains is therefore:

$$\theta_1\theta_2 = \frac{1}{UV} + \frac{2}{UV}\left(\cos 2\pi\frac{t}{U} + \cos 4\pi\frac{t}{U} + \cos 6\pi\frac{t}{U} + \ldots\right.$$

$$\left. + \cos 2\pi\frac{t}{V} + \cos 4\pi\frac{t}{V} + \cos 6\pi\frac{t}{V} + \ldots\right)$$

$$+ \frac{4}{UV}\left(\cos 2\pi\frac{t}{U}\cos 2\pi\frac{t}{V} + \cos 4\pi\frac{t}{U}\cos 2\pi\frac{t}{V} + \right.$$

$$+ \cos 2\pi\frac{t}{U}\cos 4\pi\frac{t}{V} + \cos 4\pi\frac{t}{U}\cos 4\pi\frac{t}{V} + $$

$$\left. + \cos 2\pi\frac{t}{U}\cos 6\pi\frac{t}{V} + \cos 4\pi\frac{t}{U}\cos 6\pi\frac{t}{V} + \ldots\right)$$

$$(9.11)$$

The final bracketed expression here can be expanded to give:

$$\frac{2}{UV}\left[\cos\left(\frac{1}{U}+\frac{1}{V}\right)2\pi t+\cos\left(\frac{1}{U}-\frac{1}{V}\right)2\pi t+\cos\left(\frac{2}{U}+\frac{1}{V}\right)2\pi t+\ \ldots\right.$$

$$+\cos\left(\frac{1}{U}+\frac{2}{V}\right)2\pi t+\cos\left(\frac{1}{U}-\frac{2}{V}\right)2\pi t+\cos\left(\frac{2}{U}+\frac{2}{V}\right)2\pi t+\ \ldots$$

$$+\cos\left(\frac{1}{U}+\frac{3}{V}\right)2\pi t+\cos\left(\frac{1}{U}-\frac{3}{V}\right)2\pi t+\cos\left(\frac{2}{U}+\frac{3}{V}\right)2\pi t+\ \ldots$$

$$\left.+\ \ldots\right] \tag{9.12}$$

Each term of the expansion can be written in the form:

$$\frac{2}{UV}\cos\left(\frac{a}{U}\pm\frac{b}{V}\right)2\pi t = \frac{2}{UV}\cos\left(\frac{aV\pm bU}{UV}\right)2\pi t$$

Now we know that the product wave must take the form of a single train of pulses having a pulse repetition period of UV. It can be expressed as:

$$\theta_1\theta_2 = \frac{1}{2t}\left[\frac{1}{UV}+\frac{2}{UV}\left(\cos 2\pi\frac{t}{UV}+\cos 4\pi\frac{t}{UV}+\ \ldots\right)\right] \tag{9.13}$$

It follows that in the expansion we must have

$$aV\pm bU = \text{every positive integer.}$$

It is worth noting that if the original pulse trains are A.C. coupled to a true multiplying circuit so that a true product is obtained, the first two terms of the $\theta_1\theta_2$ product expansion of equation (9.11) disappear. The final bracketed terms must therefore contain a product pulse wave, together with other negative pulses if the two pulse trains are A.C. coupled to a true multiplying circuit. However, a logical AND circuit will merely give the positive coincidence pulses without the undesired negative pulses.

It has been assumed in the above discussion that the pulses are short. If this is not so, there can be partial coincidence between several successive pulses and a true product pulse train is not obtained.

9.5 PULSE-WIDTH TOLERANCE

If the pulses used are derived by counting and gating directly from a high-frequency rectangular-wave generator, then there should be no possibility of partial coincidence between several successive pulses from two sources having different prime repetition periods. However, the

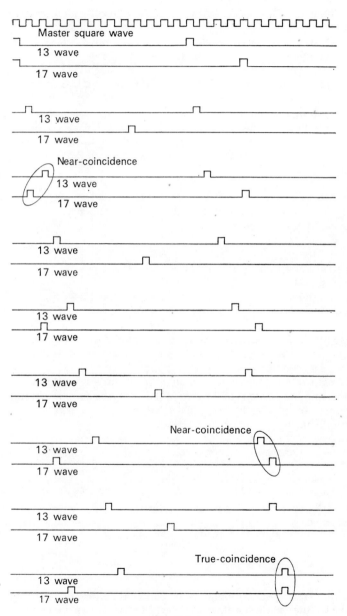

Master square wave

13 wave

17 wave

13 wave

17 wave

Near-coincidence

13 wave

17 wave

13 wave

17 wave

13 wave

17 wave

13 wave

17 wave

Near-coincidence

13 wave

17 wave

13 wave

17 wave

True-coincidence

13 wave

17 wave

Fig. 9.3

maximum usable frequency of the high-frequency rectangular wave generator will depend on the possibility of mutual interference.

Such spurious mutual interference could be caused, for example, by pulse lengthening caused by carrier storage in semiconductor elements or by the effects of stray capacitance. The difficulty is illustrated by the ringed cases in Figure 9.3 which shows two pulse trains having prime repetition periods of 13 and 17. It is seen that the pulse-width tolerance or the pulse-position tolerance is only equal to one half of the pulse width in this case. However, this is not a serious limitation, since there is no reason why shorter pulses should not be used, the master signal then not having a one-to-one mark to space ratio. With any given system this course will, however, have the result of lowering the storage capacity.

Pulses of a high carrier frequency might be used to help to overcome tape defects and also to increase the number of channels which can be carried by a given memory tape.

9.6 LIMITATIONS ON RANGE OF PULSE PERIODS

It is not practicable to arrange a system to be capable of handling pulse periods as high as: $t_a \times A \times B \times C \times \ldots X \times Y$, where $A, B, C, \ldots$ are all different prime numbers and t_a is the master pulse repetition period, since the numbers involved would become astronomical. It is therefore necessary to impose some practical limitation on the maximum number of inputs which can be associated. Suppose that it is decided that only pair-associations are to be accepted. What are the limitations on the prime numbers which can be used if there is to be an inherent rejection of pulses produced by triple associations? The rejection process is not difficult if

$$X.Y < A.B.C$$

where X and Y are the two longest prime pulse periods used (divided by the master pulse period t_a) and A, B, C, are the three shortest prime pulse periods used (again divided by t_a). In this case, the system is simply arranged to reject any pulses having a repetition period greater than $X.Y.t_a$.

The requirement $X.Y < A.B.C$ can be approximated

by $$X^2 < A^3$$

or $$X < (A^3)^{1/2}$$

i.e. the largest prime number must be less than the square root of the cube of the smallest prime number. The range can be expressed by writing:

$$X < RA$$

whence $R \approx (A)^{1/2}$ gives the approximate ratio of the largest prime number used to the smallest prime number used. However, it is also necessary to consider the distribution of prime numbers in the range in order to find how the number of available channels varies.

Now it is well known[4] that the number of primes less than any given number N is approximately equal to $N/(\ln N)$. Consequently the of number primes between A and $(A^3)^{1/2}$ is given by:

$$\frac{A\left(\frac{2}{3}(A)^{1/2} - 1\right)}{\ln A}$$

On this basis, the number of available channels increases rapidly as the value of the smallest prime number to be used is increased.

REFERENCES

1. WILLIAMS, F. C., and WEST, J. C., 'The Position Synchronisation of a Rotating Drum', *Proc. IEE*, **98,** pt. 2, 29 (1951)
2. BOOTH, A. D., 'A Magnetic Digital Storage System', *Electronic Engineering*, **21,** 234, July (1949)
3. YOUNG, J. F., and NRDC, British Provisional Patent No. 30657/68
4. BALL, W. W. R., *History of Mathematics*, Macmillan (1924)

10 | Prime Pulse Systems

The prime-period pulse system was used in one of the early learning machines[1] constructed at Aston. Non-dynamic storage was used in this machine, a loop of magnetic tape being used as the storage medium. A block diagram of this system is shown in Figure 10.1.

The input stimuli are applied to this machine by means of the switches P_1 to P_4. In order to record the association of two or more stimuli, the corresponding switches are closed coincidentally.

To achieve reliable recording of the coincidence information, the duration of the switch closure must obviously exceed the cycle time of the tape store. If, however, the closure time of the input switches is less than the cycle time, then an element of probability is introduced into the recording, and this can be a desirable feature.

10.2 PRIME PERIOD PULSE SYSTEM DESCRIPTION

In the basic prime period pulse system a loop of magnetic tape has two recording tracks. One of these (the master track) produces a continuous stream of equally spaced short pulses from a replay head. After amplification and shaping these pulses are applied to a number of electronic counters as shown in Figure 10.1. Each of these counters is designed to count repetitively a certain number of master pulses and then to give an output pulse, reset itself to zero and then to restart counting. The number of master pulses required before any particular counter gives an output pulse is arranged to be a prime number. Thus the output pulse from one counter might coincide with every 17th master pulse, another with every 29th master pulse and so on.

The output pulses from the counters can be supplied via mechanical or electronic switches to a 'Two-or-More' detector. This circuit is arranged to give an output pulse if, and only if, pulses are applied to at least two of its input terminals coincidentally. Thus if, for example,

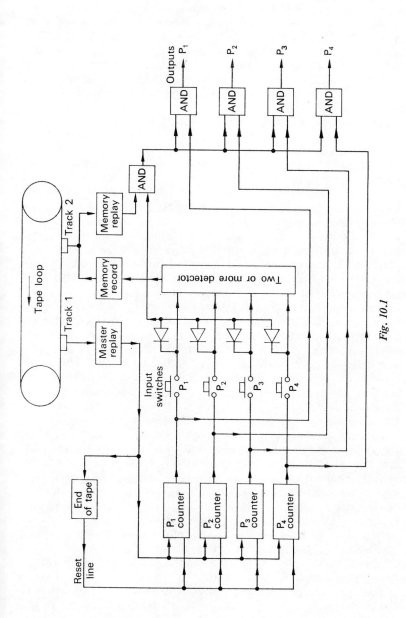

Fig. 10.1

the switch connected to the 13's counter is closed at the same time as the switch connected to the 17's counter, then the Two-or-More detector produces an output pulse coincident with every $13 \times 17 = 221$st master pulse. Now since prime numbers produce unique products, this 221 pulse can be produced by no two other input switches than the 13 and the 17 switches. Further discussion is required if it is possible for more than two switches to be energised simultaneously, and this will be dealt with later.

Any output pulse from the 'Two-or-More' detector is supplied to a recording circuit which records on the second, 'Memory', track on the tape loop. In this way, if ever two or more inputs are energised simultaneously, a unique record is made of this fact on the memory track on the tape loop.

Suppose that at some time in the past such a record has been made of two inputs, say 13 and 17, being energised simultaneously. A pulse has therefore been recorded at position 221 on the memory track, and this pulse is played back at the appropriate time each time that the correct piece of tape passes the record-playback head. Such played-back pulses are shaped and amplified and then passed to a logical AND gate. Another input to this AND gate is provided from the counters whenever one of the inputs is energised.

Now suppose, for example, that at some time in the past the 13 and the 17 inputs have been energised simultaneously, so that a pulse has been recorded on the memory track at position 221. If at the present point in time the 13 input alone is energised, then it gives out a pulse at each of the positions 13, 26, 39, ... 208, 221, 234, etc. The seventeenth pulse, at position 221, will coincide with the previously recorded pulse at this position which is now coming from the memory replay circuit. Both of these pulses are applied to the AND gate, which consequently produces an output pulse coincident with position 221.

This coincidence pulse conveys the information that the 13 and the 17 input have been energised together at some time in the past, and that at least one of them is currently being energised. The coincidence pulse is applied to a common line attached to one input of each of a further set of AND gates. The other input of each of these AND gates is supplied with pulses from one of the prime-number counters. Consequently, one of these AND gates can produce an output pulse if a pulse appears on the common line at a time position corresponding to some multiple of 13; the next requires a pulse on the common line at a position corresponding to some multiple of 17; the next some multiple of 19 and so on.

Thus if a pulse appears on the common line at position 221, then both the 13 and the 17 AND gates produce an output pulse, even though only the 13 input is at present energised. In this way, the information stored on the memory track of the recording medium about the past association of the 13 and the 17 inputs is used to produce the effect of the 17 input even though the 17 input is not at present energised.

The problems encountered in the development of a machine to operate on these principles, and the techniques adopted, are discussed in later sections.

Pulses from the master track on the magnetic recording medium are used to drive the prime-number counters producing the various prime pulses for the different input circuits. There must be a joint at some point on the tape or drum, since at some point the end of the master track recording meets the beginning of the same track. It is necessary to take steps to overcome spurious counting caused by this joint in the continuous loop of recording medium.

It should also be noted that the counters all have to count different prime numbers P_1, P_2, P_3, etc. repetitively. If all are started counting at the point where they have just produced a mutual coincidence pulse with all other counters, they will not all be in mutual coincidence again until a number $P_1 \times P_2 \times P_3 \times \ldots$ of master pulses have been produced. This would take a very long time even if very short pulse-repetition periods were used. It is not practicable or desirable to use an extremely long tape loop. Consequently it is required that all prime number counters are periodically reset to zero, and this is conveniently arranged to coincide in time with the joint in the continuous loop of recording medium. A special end-of-tape detector circuit is consequently used in order to produce the required zero-reset pulses for the counters when the joint appears.

10.3 LARGER NUMBER OF INPUTS

Suppose that a tape loop having a total capacity of N possible separate recording positions is used. With the prime-number scheme the maximum number of different available channels is given by:

$$\frac{A(\frac{2}{3}(A)^{1/2} - 1)}{\ln A}$$

where A is the smallest prime number used.

The tape capacity N is required to be approximately equal to A^3, so that the maximum number of different available channels is given by:

$$\frac{3 \times (N)^{1/3}(\frac{2}{3}(N)^{1/6} - 1)}{\ln N}$$

From this expression, even for 100 input channels the required tape storage capacity is becoming rather large.

In order to use larger numbers of inputs with the prime-number scheme, it would be necessary to have a large number of magnetic recording tracks, for example on a magnetic drum. In addition, it might be possible to use an interlaced form of storage in which, for example, the even-number spaces, which are unused in a prime-number scheme, are used to provide additional storage space.

10.4 AVOIDANCE OF SPURIOUS RESPONSE

If every coincidence of two stimulated prime number inputs is recorded, there is an additional reason for limiting the range of numbers used. Consider a coincidence of the two shortest prime input numbers used, A and B. A pulse is recorded at positions of the memory track corresponding to positions:

$$AB, 2AB, 3AB, \ldots NAB$$

on the master track. Now N might be equal to one of the prime numbers $A, B, C, \ldots$ used in the system. Suppose that $N = D$, then $NAB = DAB$. A pulse recorded at this position would falsely indicate that input D had been associated with input A and with input B. This spurious response can be avoided if the ratio of the largest prime product XY to the smallest prime product AB is less than the smallest prime A, or:

$$\frac{XY}{AB} < A$$

i.e. $$XY < A^2B$$

Approximately, this once again gives the design condition:

$$X < (A)^{3/2}$$

10.5 COINCIDENCES OF PULSE TRAINS

It is possible to consider the probabilities of obtaining coincidences between two different pulse trains by making use of that sub-division of the Theory of Numbers which deals with Linear Congruences.[3] When this is done, it is found that if there are two separate trains of pulses having pulse widths of p_1 and p_2 respectively, and repetition periods of P_1 and P_2 respectively, then in a long period of time T the two pulse trains will overlap by more than a short time of length t seconds for a fraction:

$$\frac{p_1 p_2 - t^2}{P_1 P_2} \text{ of the time } T$$

If coincidences of any width t seconds, right down to $t = 0$ seconds, are allowed, then the fractional time becomes simply equal to:

$$\frac{p_1 p_2}{P_1 P_2}$$

Thus the use of linear congruence theory leads to very simple solutions for coincidences, and it is likely that this theory will become of great importance in this field as more is learned about the significance of probability in the pulse type of association memory.

10.6 CONCLUSIONS

It has been seen that the achievment of electronic forms of neural propagation and storage of information in pulse form is quite feasible.[2] In an engineered system, the use of prime pulse periods can give economy of storage requirements, while avoiding the possibility of ambiguity of the stored association information.

With a recirculating pulse type of system, reshaping of the pulses can help to reduce the effects of cumulative distortion in the memory loop. A very close control of the effective recirculating memory loop gain is essential if it is to be ensured that the forgetting process is not to be excessively rapid. If alternative methods of forgetting can be introduced, non dynamic methods of storage can be used, thus eliminating these difficulties.

Ambiguity problems can be avoided by the use of sufficiently narrow pulses. The necessity for precise control of memory tape speed can be avoided by the use of a master pulse track on the recorder as a source of all pulses. Prime period counters are then required in order to generate the required prime period pulses from the master track.

REFERENCES

1. YOUNG, J. F., and NRDC, British Provisional Patent No. 30657/68
2. YOUNG, J. F., *Cybernetics*, Iliffe (1969)
3. MILLER, V. S., and SCHWARZ, R. J., 'On The Interference of Pulse Trains', *JAP*, **24**, 1032, Aug. (1953)

11 | The Astra Mk. 3

In the prime period pulse type of association-recording system described earlier, each input was represented by a different prime number. Such an arrangement has the advantage that all inputs are treated in exactly the same manner, regardless of the nature of the original causes of the inputs.

However, the scheme has the disadvantages that:

(1) It is wasteful of space on the magnetic tape or other storage medium, since only those points on the tape which correspond to certain prime products can be used.

(2) A separate pulse counter is required for each input. Although a method was devised whereby a standard form of counter can be used with an easily changed feedback arrangement which permits any required counting base to be adopted, the overall size of the resulting counting equipments is excessive. The use of modern forms of large scale integrated circuit could reduce the size considerably below that which was necessary in the early experimental equipment. The cost is still excessive because of the need for a number of different prime number counters.

Consequently, from an engineering viewpoint it is desirable to reduce this requirement for numbers of counters, and also to obtain a better utilisation of the space on the magnetic tape or other recording medium. Both of these deficiencies of the earlier scheme were overcome by the development of the newer scheme, which has been called the ASTRA Mk. 3 machine.[1]

The new arrangement can be described with reference to Figure 11.1. Only a single master pulse counter is now required. For convenience this counter can be of the decimal type and it can have several stages, though there is in fact no limitation on the the base of the counter, a binary or a duodecimal base being equally usable.

In Figure 11.1, the inputs are indicated as coming from switches,

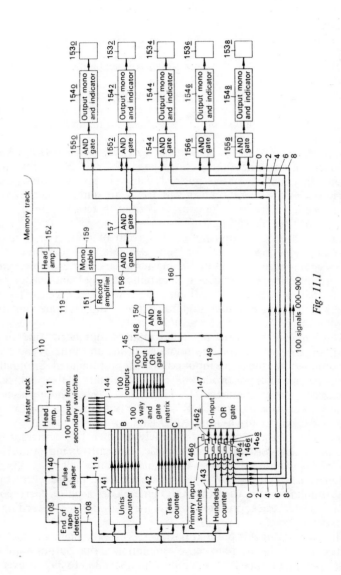

Fig. 11.1

though these could equally well be electronic switches operated from, for example, photo-electric devices or sound-actuated devices.

On the ASTRA Mk. 3 scheme, the inputs are divided into two groups:

(1) Those 'reflex' inputs which operate an output 'muscle' whenever they are stimulated.

(2) Those 'conditioned' inputs which are incapable of operating any output directly.

It is the function of the machine to enable each particular member of the second group of inputs to operate an output muscle only provided that this output has in the past been stimulated coincidentally with the presently existing input.

In order to illustrate the principle of operation of the ASTRA Mk. 3 arrangement, assume that a three-stage decimal counter is used, capable of counting master pulses repetitively up to a total of 999, and repeating the operation over and over again until, when the master pulses cease occurrence, the counter is reset to zero by the action of the 'end-of-tape' detector.

The occurrence of any one of the group of reflex inputs passes a signal to one input of the 10-input OR gate. The duration of any such signal is equal to that of 100 master pulses. For example, one of this group of inputs produces a long pulse lasting from master pulse 300 to master pulse 399. This long pulse can in fact take the form of a train of 100 shorter pulses, and utilisation of this fact can sometimes simplify the rest of the equipment.

Now suppose that while this reflex input is stimulated, one of the conditioned or nerve inputs is stimulated at the same time. As an example, suppose that the nerve input number 27 is stimulated. Stimulation of this particular input produces, from the counter, pulses coinciding with master pulses numbers 027, 127, 227, ... 927. These pulses are all also taken to a 100-input OR gate. The outputs from the two OR gates are taken to a two-input AND gate.

Only one of the nerve pulses, namely number 327, coincides with that previously-postulated reflex pulse, currently being stimulated, which lasts from master pulse 300 to master pulse 399.

Consequently, if the two inputs postulated are indeed ever stimulated simultaneously, then the AND gate passes a pulse corresponding to master track position 327 to the recorder for recording on the memory track.

The presence of this pulse at position 327 on the memory track can then be used in the future to cause stimulation of that output number 3 (corresponding to master track pulses numbers 300 to 399) if ever the nerve input number 27 (corresponding to master track pulses numbers 027, 127, 227, ... 927) is again stimulated, even though the reflex input number 3 is not then at that time being stimulated.

An earlier simultaneous stimulation of any reflex input coincidentally with any nerve input then makes it possible for that nerve input to stimulate that particular corresponding muscle output at any time in the future.

11.2 PROBABILISTIC RECORDING

The methods of association recording which have been considered were developed while keeping in mind the possible need for the future introduction of various features. It was considered to be important not to prevent the later introduction of these features by, for example, adopting inflexible methods of information storage.

In order to introduce the feature of probability into the recording method, it is required that the occurrence of any single association between inputs shall not necessarily saturate the section of memory store reserved for that particular association. Instead, it is required that the more frequently that a particular association between any two inputs has occurred in the past, then the more likely it is in the future that one alone of the two inputs is able to stimulate the output corresponding to the other input.

One way of producing this feature is by the introduction of a random perturbation of the position at which the pulses corresponding to any particular association are recorded on the magnetic memory medium. The more often that a particular association has occurred in the past, then the greater will be the density of pulses recorded around the corresponding tape position and the greater will be the probability that a future pulse occurring in that nominal position will correspond to one of the previously recorded pulses.

The required random perturbation could be introduced, for example, by production of a random variation of the speed of the recording medium. Alternatively, electronic methods of random position perturbation could be introduced, and this method has received most attention at Aston.

A simple method of introducing a random perturbation in the system of the ASTRA Mk. 3 machine has been developed by Marklew at Aston. The pulse produced by any particular conditioned or nerve input causes a monostable circuit to trip. However, no pulse is passed on to the rest of the ASTRA circuit until a further pulse is received, this time from a source of random, or of quasi-random pulses. By inserting the delay circuit at a suitable point in the association circuitry, only a single random delay unit is required.

11.3 FORGETTING

Forgetting is another feature which, like probabilistic recording, was kept in mind during the development of the ASTRA machines, so that the possibility of its later introduction would not be ruled out by the nature of the methods considered for adoption.

There are several methods by which the forgetting feature might be introduced. One of these depends on the slow partial decay of the information stored on a magnetic medium which can occur when a small high frequency magnetic erase field is applied to the tape. Repetition of such partial decay leads to an effective gradual decay of stored information. This effect was noted by Hollingshead during work on the ASTRA system at Aston, and proposed for use in the forgetting mechanism.

If the information is stored in the form of short pulses on a magnetic medium, one possibility which can be used to introduce the feature of forgetting is the imposition of short random erase pulses. These can be applied to a magnetic recording head in the opposite direction to that used for the record pulses. Such random pulses would have the effect of introducing random erasure and so of causing a random forgetting of stored information.

If the recorded pulses have a random position distribution about the correct points on the recording medium, then the erasing pulses should also have a random distribution of position. The forgetting erasure pulses will then take longer to erase completely a memory of any association which has occurred very frequently in the past than to erase the memory of a single past association.

It has been suggested by Wilkins[2] that the rate of forgetting should not be constant for all elements in a nervous system. The elements concerned with fine detail should have a faster rate of forgetting than have those concerned with broader areas. This might explain the observed loss of accuracy which precedes a total loss of memory. This sort of effect could be obtained either if different elements had different forgetting time constants or if the elements had the same time constants but different thresholds.

It should perhaps be mentioned that if a forgetting action is to be accomplished by the imposition of random negative pulses, then the normal condition of the recording medium should be a state of negative saturation. On the application of a record pulse, the medium is then taken to positive saturation. On the application of a negative, erasure, forgetting random pulse, the recording medium is then returned to a state of negative saturation, from which it started originally. Such a system is inherently insensitive to noise, though it does need large pulse amplitudes.

In the course of his work on computer simulation of the ASTRA system at Aston, Fisher has made the interesting observation that subtraction of a constant amount from all stored memories has the effect of contrast enhancement. The basic reason for this is that once a stored signal is reduced to zero, it cannot be further reduced, so that successive subtractions tend to leave only the peaks of remembered information. Thus, forgetting using such a technique would enhance the contrast of memories, by emphasising the peaks.

11.4 INHIBITION

There are two forms of inhibition which must be considered for possible introduction into associatory learning machines. For one form, it is required that the occurrence of certain inputs should be capable of being associated with the stimulation of definite inhibiting outputs. As an example, in the human arm the triceps muscles are opposed by the biceps muscles, and it is necessary to inhibit the action of one set when the other set are stimulated.

This is a quite straight-forward operation, simply requiring inter-coupling of the control systems of the opposing sets of muscles in order to prevent their simultaneous excitation. The action can take place externally to any associating machine which provides the prime control.

However, a second form of inhibition may be active at a lower level of nervous activity. Observation of the action of living nerve cells indicates that certain synaptic inputs to some cells appear to be capable of inhibiting the output from that cell. If this is so, then such inhibition might well be capable of direct reduction of stored memory levels. This is conjectural, though it does appear to agree with observation at a molar level.

It is consequently desirable that the possibility of later introduction of active direct inhibitory association should be catered for. This can, for example, take the form of pulses recorded or applied to the record head in the reverse direction.

11.5 FRACTIONAL TIME ERRORS

In order that there shall be no confusion between pulses, although a time error is both desirable and inescapable in the present application, this error must have a maximum value which is less than the minimum time between pulses.

Assume that the time variation of pulses is $\pm t$. Then the minimum time between pulses is $T_1 - 2t$, where T_1 is the normal pulse interval.

Also assume that the speed variation of the recording medium can be expressed as:

$$v = V_1(1+f(t))$$

The minimum distance between recorded pulses on the recording medium is then given by:

$$d_m = (T_1 - 2t)V_1(1 - f'(t))$$

where $f'(t)$ is the peak v alue of $f(t)$.

Now when these two pulses are reproduced, let the variation of velocity of the recording medium be expressed by:

$$v = V_2(1+g(t))$$

Then the minimum reproduced time interval T_2 between two pulses will be given by:

$$T_{2m} = \frac{d_m}{V_2(1+g'(t))}$$

where $g'(t)$ is the peak value of $g(t)$.

Substituting in the value of d_m:

$$T_{2m} = (T_1 - 2t) \cdot \frac{V_1(1-f'(t))}{V_2(1+g'(t))}$$

It will be seen from this that if $f'(t)$ and $g'(t)$ are both small and if $V_1 = V_2$, then the maximum error per pulse is t, as would be expected. However, if this is not so, then there is an additional time error.

The maximum fractional time error can be expressed as:

$$\frac{T_1 - T_{2m}}{T_1} = 1 - \frac{T_{2m}}{T_1}$$

This becomes:

$$1 - \frac{T_1 - 2t}{T_1} \cdot \frac{V_1(1-f'(t))}{V_2(1+g'(t))}$$

$$= \frac{T_1(V_2(1+g'(t))) - V_1(1-f'(t)) + 2tV_1(1-f'(t))}{T_1V_2(1+g'(t))}$$

It should be noted here that if $V_1 = V_2$, as can normally be expected, then:

$$\text{Max. error} = \frac{T_1(f'(t)+g'(t)) + 2t(1+f'(t))}{T_1(1+g'(t))}$$

Furthermore, if $f'(t) = g'(t)$ in addition, then:

$$\text{Max. error} = \frac{2f'(t)}{1+f'(t)} + \frac{2t}{T_1} \cdot \frac{(1-f'(t))}{(1+f'(t))}$$

expressed as a fraction of the normal pulse interval.
This approximation can be written as:

$$\text{Max. error} = \frac{2f'(t)}{1+f'(t)} \left[1 - \frac{2t}{T_1} \right] + \frac{2t}{T_1}$$

For values of $f'(t)$ up to $0\cdot1$, the convenient approximation can be used:

$$\frac{2f'(t)}{1+f'(t)} \approx 1\cdot8f'(t)$$

In general, it is required that the maximum error is equal to some constant fraction of T_1, say kT. Hence:

$$1 - \frac{T_1 - 2t}{T_1} \cdot \frac{V_1(1-f'(t))}{V_2(1+g'(t))} = k$$

From this, it follows that:

$$t = \frac{T_1}{2} \left[1 - (1-k) \frac{V_2(1+g'(t))}{V_1(1-f'(t))} \right]$$

Thus, given the mechanical drive characteristics of the recording medium, it is possible to determine the required amount of time variation for a given error function k.

11.6 MULTIPLE ASSOCIATION MACHINES

It is clear that in biological mechanisms, the number of input nerve cells is vastly in excess of the number of output muscles. Now with an extendible associating-machine of the ASTRA type, the number of storage locations required is equal to the product:

Storage Locations = Number of Inputs×Number of Outputs

Consider a simple machine of the ASTRA type, having 1000 input nerves and 100 muscle outputs. Then the storage capacity required in the simple ASTRA machine is 100 000 store locations. Furthermore, the time required to search through and recirculate the simple ASTRA store will be 100 000 t, where t is the time required per storage location.

If such a system was adopted by the animal control system, then not only would a very large storage capacity be required, but the response would be very slow. In the latter connection, of course, the animal system probably operates on a majority basis rather than on a serial search basis.

The animal nervous system appears to be much more sub-divided than is the simple scheme discussed above. Sub-systems operate into the main system as though they were each single inputs to the main system. It is therefore of interest to consider the possibility of the adoption of such a hierarchical system with the ASTRA machines.

Suppose a simple machine such as ASTRA Mk. 3, having 100 nerve inputs and 10 muscle outputs, is used in conjunction with 100 similar machines, each of which has only one output which provides one of the inputs to the main machine.

With such a hierarchical ASTRA system, the total storage requirement is equal to:

Total = Subsidiary Machines + Main Machine

$$= 100 \times 100 \text{ locations} + 1000 \text{ locations}$$

$$= 11\ 000 \text{ locations}$$

This compares with 100 000 locations for the simple form of ASTRA.

Furthermore, the search and recirculate time for the hierarchical system is only equal to 1100 t.

To generalise this argument, if:

M_1 = Number of muscle outputs from main machine

M_2 = Number of muscle outputs from subsidiary machine

n_1 = Number of nerve inputs to main machine

n_2 = Number of nerve inputs to each subsidiary machine

Then for a two-stage system as described, the ratio:

$$\frac{\text{Store capacity of serial ASTRAs}}{\text{Store capacity of single ASTRA}} = \frac{M_2}{M_1} \left(1 + \frac{M_1}{n_2} \right)$$

For a three-stage hierarchical machine, the ratio becomes:

$$\frac{\text{Serial store}}{\text{Single store}} = \frac{M_3}{M_1} \left(1 + \frac{M_2}{n_3} + \frac{M_2 M_1}{n_3 n_2} \right)$$

This form of relationship can be continued for a machine having more than three stages.

However, in general the number of outputs is much smaller than the number of inputs, so that as a first approximation it can be said that the ratio is:

$$\frac{\text{Number of first-stage outputs } M_x}{\text{Number of final (muscle) outputs } M_1}$$

This ratio could typically be 1/100.
The argument in this form is due to Fisher of Aston.

REFERENCES

1. YOUNG, J. F., and NRDC, British Provisional Patent No. 30657/68
2. WILKINS, B. R., 'Memory and Learning Circuits', *Industrial Electronics*, **1**, 96 and 154 Nov/Dec. (1962)

12 | Information Storage

12.1 MAGNETIC PULSE RECORDING

Those methods of recording short pulses on magnetic tape which have been used in digital computer storage systems[1] are not necessarily automatically applicable to cybernetic memory systems.

If it is required that new information can easily be added to the information impressed earlier on the recording medium, at all positions on the medium, then RZ or Return-to-Zero based methods are desirable. Unfortunately, the minimum permissible spacing between adjacent recorded signals is greater with this system than with some other systems. This fact is often expressed by the statement that the maximum bit density of this system is low.

In an attempt to optimise the storage, it is necessary first to consider the effect of bit-density variation in the particular form of magnetic recording used in an association memory system.

The pulses of information to be stored are applied to the record head via capacitor from an amplifier which is capable of supplying high-voltage record pulses to an inductive load.

If the voltage applied via a capacitor to the recording head has a rectangular waveform, then the current flows in two opposing quasi-differential spikes. If these current spikes have sufficient amplitude to take the recording medium into saturation, then the magnetisation of the recording medium takes the form of two opposing pulses which can be considered as a first approximation to be rectangular. When a tape having this magnetisation moves past a replay head, the resulting output voltage takes the form of two opposing bipolar pulses.

If the applied recording pulse is progressively narrowed, the two output voltage pulses approach until they combine into a single larger amplitude negative pulse. It is then of interest to consider whether there is any optimum width of recording pulse of voltage.

It is usual to assume that the read-head voltage response produced by a step change of tape magnetisation can be approximated by a Gaussian function:

$$f(t) = \exp(-t^2) \qquad (12.1)$$

This proves in practice to be a reasonable approximation. Now if we have two adjacent step-changes in opposite directions, the read pulse is approximated by

$$f(t) = \exp(-t^2) - \exp(-(t-x)^2) \qquad (12.2)$$

where x is the time between the step changes. If we have four adjacent step changes in $+$, $-$, $-$, $+$ directions, the read pulses are approximated by:

$$f(t) = \exp(-t^2) - \exp(-(t-x)^2) - \exp(-(t-T)^2)$$
$$+ \exp(-(t-x-T)^2) \qquad (12.3)$$

In the case under consideration, x is the width of the magnetising pulses, while T is the width of the applied voltage pulse.

It is required to find the optimum value of T, with x fixed, to give a maximum amplitude of read pulse. Consider the amplitude at the mid-point where $t = \frac{1}{2}(T+x)$. Substitution of this value into equation (12.3) shows that the maximum amplitude is given by:

$$f_{max}(t) = -4 \exp\left(\frac{1}{4}(T^2+x^2)\right) \times \sinh \frac{1}{2}Tx \qquad (12.4)$$

It can be assumed that x is fixed at the shortest possible value. Now put $T = kx$, then:

$$f_{max}(t) = -4 \exp\left(-\frac{1}{4}(k^2+1)\right)x^2 \times \sinh \frac{1}{2}kx^2 \qquad (12.5)$$

In Figure 12.1, $f_{max}(t)$ is plotted against the value of k. It is seen that there is a maximum value at $k = 1\cdot5$. The maximum value is given by:

$$f_{max}(t) = 2[\exp(-1\cdot56x^2) - \exp(-0\cdot56x^2)] \qquad (12.6)$$

If the value of x is taken as unity, then evaluation of equation (12.6) gives:

$$f_{max}(t) = -1\cdot46 \qquad (12.7)$$

It has been shown above that the optimum pulse width is given by $T = 1\cdot5x$, if maximum peak amplitude is taken as the criterion. It is of interest to examine the way in which the actual shape of the read pulse changes as the value of T/x is varied. Curves showing the pulse shape for various values of T/x, as calculated from equation (3), are given in Figures 12.2 and 12.3.

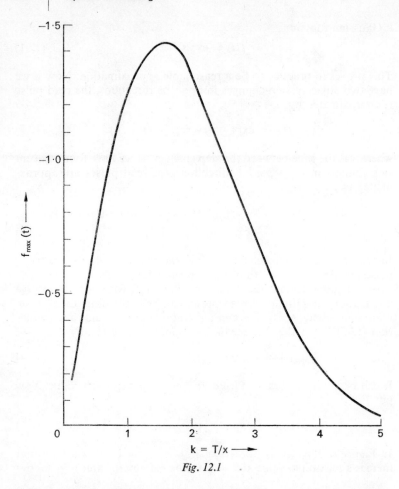

Fig. 12.1

In practice, the positive part of the waveform can easily be eliminated, for example by diode switching. It is then of interest to examine the behaviour of the ratio:

$$\frac{\text{Negative Peak Amplitude}}{\text{Distance Between Zeros}}$$

and to use this ratio as a figure of merit as the value of T is varied. The figure of merit varies with the value of $k = T/x$ as shown in Figure 12.4.

The preceding analysis is of use for well-designed digital magnetic recorders having low-inductance head windings. It is possible to make

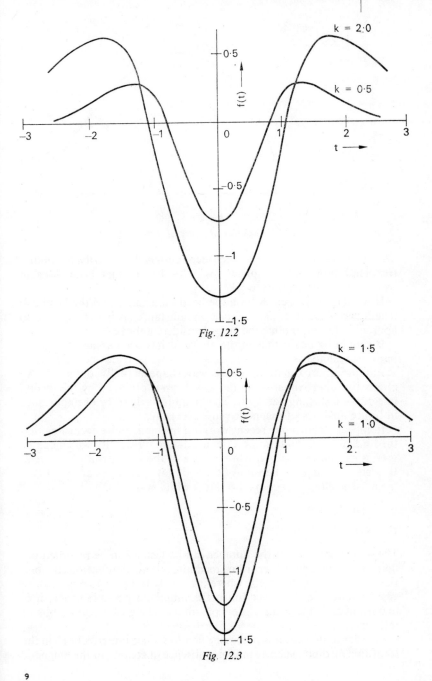

Fig. 12.2

Fig. 12.3

9

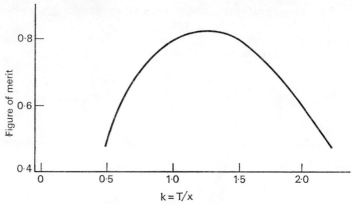

Fig. 12.4 Variation of figure of merit with k

use of simple low-frequency recorders designed primarily for audio-frequency, non pulse applications. This has in fact been done in some cybernetic memory work.

However, in such cases both the head inductance and the head gap lengths are excessive, and in such circumstances it is not possible to approach the optimum conditions considered above.

It should be noted that in the above, it has been assumed that the basic waveshape is Gaussian. However, this provides no more than a suitable approximation to the waveshape actually obtained. An alternative approximation to the waveform is provided by the second integral of a rectangular wave. This point is likely to be of importance in future analyses of magnetic pulse recording.

It appears from some recent work on magnetic pulse recording that the fundamental limitation on the maximum bit-density which can be used is caused by the non white nature of the noise from the system. It is claimed that bit densities of 10 000 bits per inch can be used if the noise is filtered to convert it into a white noise.

12.2 INCREASE OF BIT DENSITY

The bit density, that is the number of bits which can be recorded per unit length of magnetic recording medium, is limited by various factors. For cybernetic applications, where it is likely to be necessary to store vast quantities of information in the minimum possible space, it is important to achieve the closest possible packing of recorded bits of information.

In order to do this, it is necessary first to reduce imperfections in the recording medium, such as pinpoint absence of coating of the magnetic material, since these can cause 'drop-outs' of information. Attention must also be given to the design of the recording and reproducing heads on the recording device, since imperfections here such as field asymmetry can have the effect of limiting the maximum achievable bit-density, as well as of producing a poor reproduced pulse shape.

If attention is given to the actual shape of an output pulse obtained from a magnetic recording system, then it is found that the waveshape is asymmetrical. The asymmetry is due to various causes, but it can be treated as a phase distortion effect from the signal equalisation point of view.

Methods of pulse-width reduction which have been proposed vary in their complexity.[2, 6] A very complex approach is neither desirable nor necessary in cybernetics applications, especially to mobile robots. Consequently, the approach used at Aston has been a fairly simple one incorporating integrated circuits. The design used by Yee will be described here.

12.3 SIGNAL EQUALISATION

If a pulse having the form of a time function

$$f_1(t) = \exp(-t^2)$$

is considered, then this corresponds to a function the variation of which with frequency is given by:

$$F_1(\omega) = \exp(-\tfrac{1}{4}\omega^2)$$

where multiplicative constants are ignored.

Now it is required to operate on this frequency function, by making use of an electronic circuit, in order to produce a pulse of narrower width:

$$f_2(t) = \exp(-a^2 t^2)$$

where $a > 1$.

This pulse corresponds to a frequency function:

$$F_2(\omega) = \exp\left(-\frac{\omega^2}{4a^2}\right)$$

Then to convert $F_1(\omega)$ to $F_2(\omega)$, we must multiply by:

$$\frac{F_2(\omega)}{F_1(\omega)} = \exp\left(1 - \frac{1}{a^2}\right)\frac{\omega^2}{4}$$

This then gives the required frequency characteristic of a network which would act on the pulse in such a way as to cause it to be narrowed.

As an example, consider $a = (2)^{1/2}$ so that $a^2 = 2$ and $f_2(t) = \exp(-2t^2)$. The pulses $f_1(t)$ and $f_2(t)$ have an amplitude-time response

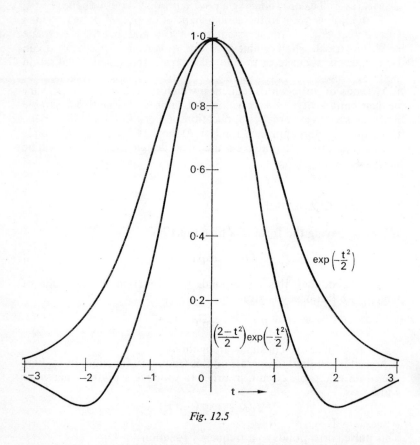

Fig. 12.5

such that $f_2(t)$ is narrower than $f_1(t)$. The required frequency characteristic of a network to achieve this narrowing would be:

$$\frac{F_2(\omega)}{F_1(\omega)} = \exp\left(\frac{\omega^2}{8}\right)$$

This would require the use of a network which had a gain which increased sharply with frequency. Various methods of approaching the required characteristic have been proposed.

12.4 SIMPLE PULSE EQUALISATION FOR ROBOT MEMORIES

It is convenient here to assume that a pulse has a normalised Gaussian waveshape:

$$f_1(t) = \exp\left(-\tfrac{1}{2}t^2\right)$$

Then the rate of change of the pulse with time is:

$$f_1'(t) = -t \exp\left(-\tfrac{1}{2}t^2\right)$$

and the second differential is given by:

$$f_1''(t) = (t^2 - 1)\exp\left(-\tfrac{1}{2}t^2\right)$$

These functions are plotted against time in Figure 12.5.

Now suppose that the pulse $f_1(t)$ is applied to a correcting network having the response:

$$\frac{V_0}{V_1} = 1 + \omega^2 X^2 = 1 - (j\omega)^2 X^2$$

where ω is the natural frequency.

The response can then be expressed in differential form as:

$$V_0 = V_1 - X^2 \frac{d_2 V_1}{dt^2}$$

Consequently, if the pulse having a Gaussian waveshape is applied to this network, then the output pulse becomes:

$$V_0 = \exp\left(-\tfrac{1}{2}t^2\right) - X^2(t^2 - 1)\exp\left(-\tfrac{1}{2}t^2\right)$$
$$= \exp\left(\tfrac{1}{2} - t^2\right)(1 + X^2 - X^2 t^2)$$

and if, for convenience, $X = 1$, then:

$$V_0 = (2 - t^2)\exp\left(-\tfrac{1}{2}t^2\right)$$

A pulse having one half of this pulse amplitude is plotted for comparison with the original pulse in equation (12.5). It can be seen that a network having this V_0/V_1 response can narrow the pulse.

12.5 CIRCUIT FOR CORRECTING NETWORK

It can be seen that the network having the $(1 + \omega^2 X^2)$ response could be used to narrow down the width of a Gaussian pulse. In order to show how this response can be obtained, it is first expressed as:

$$1 + \omega^2 X^2 = (1 + j\omega X)(1 - j\omega X)$$

Then if two networks having the responses $(1+j\omega X)$ and $(1-j\omega X)$ are cascaded, the overall transfer function required will be obtained.

A suitable arrangement is shown in Figure 12.6. Here, an emitter follower stage is used to give a low source impedance to the next stage. The second stage is an operational amplifier which gives the response:

$$\frac{V_{02}}{V_{i2}} = -\frac{R_2}{R_1}(1+j\omega C R_1)$$

It is more difficult to obtain the remaining term of the transfer function which is required. It has been obtained by making use of an operational amplifier which has differential inputs, as shown in the third stage of Figure 12.6.

Circuits such as this certainly have the effect if sharpening the pulses, and more complex forms have been used. Some of these are very critical to the speed of movement of the magnetic medium, others are not. Sometimes phase compensation is separately included. For some applications at Aston, a simple resonant circuit has been found adequate for pulse sharpening. The particular method to be used can only be determined from a careful consideration of the particular application.

12.6 ERASE SUPPLY

For experimental work using a magnetic recorder, some method of erasure of the recordings is necessary. The classical method of using a sinusoidal voltage applied to the erase head can be used. However, although it is undesirable to use thermionic valves in the high-frequency supply, it is also necessary to produce the high frequency sinusoid at a high voltage. This is because the erase head has an appreciable inductance, and in order to ensure that an adequate erase current is supplied it is necessary for the applied voltage to be high.

High voltage transistors, operating on a 240 volt supply, have been used for this at Aston. Since the writer has in the past developed new forms of oscillator from the well-known Wien Bridge type,[7] this form was first used with the incorporation of an integrated-circuit form of amplifier. However, difficulties with the control of amplitude were encountered, and these led to distortion of the erase voltage waveform. It is possible to use non frequency-sensitive devices such as Zener diodes in the amplitude control circuits of *RC* oscillators using a low-pass *RC* filter as the frequency-determining elements.[8] However, these are not suitable for use with the Wien or the *RCCR* bridge oscillator, because of the low attenuation at harmonic frequencies.

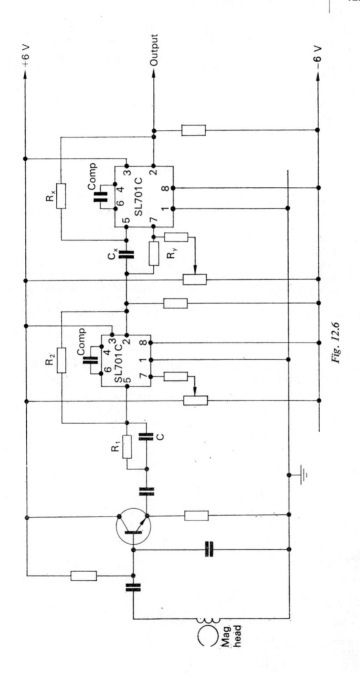

Fig. 12.6

It was then realised that the difficulty could be overcome by simply resonating the erase head with series and shunt capacitors.

This approach was so successful that eventually it was found to be possible to use a simple integrated circuit form of multi-vibrator square wave high-frequency erase oscillator, and to reduce the harmonic content of the erase current by simply resonating the erase head with capacitors.

This work was done in Aston by Lee and Zinyowera.

REFERENCES

1. HOAGLAND, A. A., *Digital Magnetic Recording*, Wiley (1963)
2. DENNISON, R. C., 'Aperture Compensation for Television Pick-Up Equipment', *Proc. NEC*, **9**, 567 (1953)
3. DENNISON, R. C., 'Aperture Compensation for Television Cameras', *RCA Rev.*, **14**, 569 Dec. (1953)
4. SIERRA, H. M., 'Increased Magnetic Recording Readback Resolution by means of Passive Network', *IBMJ*, 4, 22, Jan. (1963)
5. SIERRA, H. M., 'Bit Shift and Crowding in Digital Magnetic Recording', *Electrotechnology*, 56, Sep. (1966)
6. JACOBY, G. V., 'Signal Equalisation in Digital Magnetic Recording', *Trans. IEEE*, **4**, 302, Sept. (1968)
7. YOUNG, J. F., 'Alternatives to the Wien Bridge', *Wireless World*, **65**, 92, Feb. (1959)
8. YOUNG, J. F., 'A Simple Very Low Frequency Oscillator', *Electronic Engineering*, **31**, 218, April (1959)

13 | Counters

13.1 THE REQUIREMENT FOR COUNTERS

In the cybernetic associating-machines investigated at Aston, there has been a requirement for various forms of pulse counter. In early work, large numbers of counters, each capable of division by a different prime number, were required. In such a case, there were two outstanding requirements:

(1) The counters must be inexpensive, since numbers of them are required.
(2) The counters must be easy to set-up to count any required number.

The counter inputs are to be drawn from a master pulse source common to all counters. The prime-number output from each of the counters has to be used to drive a number of gates of various types.

A number of different counting techniques have been used in the course of the work, and since some of the work has led to new forms of circuitry it is worth describing briefly here. Like much of the work at Aston it has found applications in other fields than the cybernetic engineering, for which it was originally intended.

13.2 PULSE COUNTERS

Various forms of pulse counter have been used in the work described here. In early work, dekatron cold-cathode tubes were used in the counter circuits, following earlier satisfactory experience of their use not only in the conventional counter circuits but also as step-waveform generators.[1] New methods of coupling, using high-voltage transistors, were developed, and the early dekatron counters used on ASTRA incorporated these methods.[3] However, it proved to be difficult to obtain dekatron tubes, and so transistor forms of counter had to be used.

These were based on the form of counter developed by the writer to make use of transistor static switching units.[2] However, this form is best suited for use with an even base of counting, and a standardised form of counter was required which could easily be set to count to any required base.

The form developed incorporated integrated circuits. It was arranged to be easily set to count to any required base by inserting plugs into the front panel, prime counting bases being required in the early work.

Finally, in later work on ASTRA Mk. 3, simple decimal counters were required, and commercial transistorised units, incorporating numerical indicator tubes, were used.

13.3 DEKATRON COUNTERS

The use of multi-output decimal or duodecimal counters such as trochotrons or dekatrons is attractive, since this would limit the number of inputs to *AND* gates required in deriving the prime-number sources. Trochotrons can be used to count at a comparatively fast rate, but they are expensive and their use would necessitate the provision of a heater supply.

Cold cathode dekatron tubes claimed to be capable of a 50 kHz counting rate were available for a time. It was decided to avoid the use of these relatively untried tubes, and this proved later to have been the correct decision.

There was no reason why the initial work should not be carried out using a fairly low value of pulse repetition frequency. For example, if a 30 inch tape loop was operated at a speed of $7\frac{1}{2}$ inches per second, and the master track contained 10 000 pulses, then the pulse rate would be only 2500 bits per second at a spacing of 333 bits per inch. If a 3 : 1 duty ratio is assumed, then the pulses would be 0·1 msec long, spaced by 0·4 msec. The counting of such pulses is within the capabilities of normal dekatron selector tubes.

13.4 COUPLING DEKATRONS USING LOW-VOLTAGE TRANSISTORS

Dekatron coupling arrangements using cold cathode triodes have the disadvantage of a limited speed of operation, while those using hot cathode valves have all the disadvantages associated with the necessity for heating. Consequently, there have been various attempts to use transistors to couple dekatron stages.

Of necessity, early methods of coupling dekatron stages using transistors incorporated low-voltage transistors driving step-up transformers to increase the amplitude of the pulses to a suitable level for application to dekatron guides. The circuits used[4] were based on the use of a form of electronic curcuit known as the blocking oscillator.

A typical circuit[4] is shown in Figure 13.1. The *pnp* transistor is normally biased to the 'off' condition, and its collector is therefore at a voltage of -12 V. Since the diode D_1 is connected to a voltage

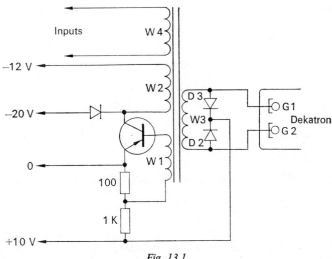

Fig. 13.1

of -20 V, it does not conduct at this time. If an input pulse is applied to the winding W_4 on the coupling transformer, the transistor base is driven negatively by transformer action and the transistor conducts. Consequently, a voltage of 12 volts appears across the winding W_2 of the transformer, and the current in this winding builds up. The transistor is held in the conducting state in the meantime by the induced voltage appearing across winding W_1.

When the build-up of current in the winding W_2 ceases, then the induced e.m.f. in winding W_1 disappears and the transistor cuts off. The reduction of collector current flowing in the winding W_2 causes the voltage appearing across that winding to reverse, so increasing the collector voltage of the transistor past the level of 12 volts. However, the collector voltage is prevented from exceeding 20 volts because the diode D_1 conducts at this level.

Thus, each time that the transistor is triggered into the 'on' condition, a bipolar form of pulse appears at its collector, which goes from -12 volts, to zero, then to -20 volts, then back to -12 volts. This bipolar pulse appears across all windings of the transformer.

Winding W_3 of the transformer is connected to the guides of the dekatron counter tube, and it has enough turns on this winding to produce about 100 volts. The diodes D_2 and D_3 in this circuit have the effect of clamping one end or the other end of the winding W_3 to the voltage $+10$, the end clamped depending on the voltage polarity appearing across the winding.

The ends of the winding are connected to guides 1 and 2 of the dekatron counter tube. The polarity of connection of winding W_3 is arranged so that when the transistor conducts, diode D_3 conducts and guide 1 is taken negative, so that the dekatron glow transfers to guide 1. Then, when the transistor cuts off, the voltage across the transformer reverses so that diode D_2 conducts and guide 2 of the dekatron is taken negative. The glow then transfers from guide 1 to guide 2. Finally, the voltage across the transformer winding disappears, both guides return to a voltage of $+10$ volts and the dekatron glow moves to the next cathode. The glow then rests until the next pulse is applied to winding W_4 of the transformer.

13.5 COUPLING DEKATRON SELECTORS USING TRANSISTORS ONLY

When higher-voltage transistors became available, attempts were made to dispense with the coupling pulse-transformer used in earlier designs with low-voltage transistors. One published method appears to be incomplete in that there is no normal form of D.C. return path in the transistor base circuit at all.[5] Such circuits should be avoided. A more controlled design[6] using the same transistors was described by Fraser. For interstage coupling of dekatron counter tubes a single high-voltage transistor was used with a 105 volt collector supply, connected in a circuit reminiscent of some of those used with early cold cathode tube coupling arrangements.

In the input stage two transistors were used, one for each guide electrode of the dekatron, with a certain amount of positive feedback from the collector of the second to the base of the first. This helped to reduce the length of the trailing edge of the first transfer pulse, and it decreased the rise time of the second transfer pulse. These circuits are stated to be very satisfactory for use with medium-speed counters.

More recently, very low cost *npn* transistors rated at 120 volts became available. Such devices are ideally suited to Dekatron coupling applications, though they are actually intended to drive cold cathode numerical indicator tubes.

One circuit investigated[3] for use with such transistors is shown in Figure 13.2. The transistor is normally biased to the non conducting condition by the forward drop of the diode in the emitter circuit, since the base is connected via a resistor to the negative supply line. However, a positive input pulse can overcome the bias and so cause forward base current to flow. When this happens, the transistor conducts and a negative pulse, of amplitude nearly equal to the supply

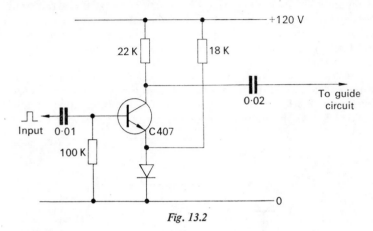

Fig. 13.2

voltage, appears at the collector. This pulse is coupled to the conventional guide circuit via a capacitor, a D.C. restoring diode being included.

While this arrangement proved reasonably satisfactory for use with dekatron selectors, the amplitude of the output pulse was not really adequate to give reliable operation of selectors over a wide range of possible repetition frequencies. However, it would probably be adequate for use with medium-speed counter tubes. Unfortunately, the size of the output pulse is limited by the maximum collector voltage rating of the transistor, and it could not be increased without risk of unreliability.

The cost of these transistors is so low compared with that of the dekatron selector that the possibility of using two transistors in each coupling circuit need not be dismissed on economic grounds. It is therefore possible, as mentioned earlier, to consider the use of the cascade arrangement for coupling, using two high-voltage low-cost transistors per stage.

The method used actually makes use of a property of a form of common base transistor circuit which has been called the voltage-doubling arrangement. For pulse applications, this arrangement is capable of giving an output voltage amplitude of twice the voltage rating of the transistors used, and so it is ideal for consideration in the present application.

13.6 VOLTAGE-DOUBLING COMMON-BASE ARRANGEMENT

The voltage-doubling arrangement for obtaining an output pulse amplitude equal to twice the voltage rating of the transistor is shown in Figure 13.3. It should perhaps be mentioned that this arrangement can equally well be used to increase the effective voltage rating of a thermionic triode or, more importantly, of a field-effect transistor of the junction type, but the analysis here will be given in terms of the junction transistor.

The transistor is in the common-base connection, the input going to the emitter while the base is biased from the two resistors R across the supply V_s. If the transistor is cut-off, no voltage appears across the load R_L. As the emitter is made negative to the base, the transistor

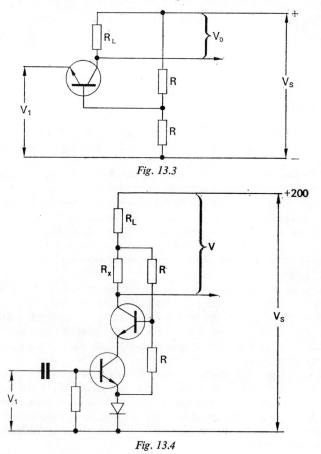

Fig. 13.3

Fig. 13.4

starts to conduct and the output voltage V_0 increases. When the output voltage has increased to rather over one-half of the supply voltage, then the collector-to-base voltage of the transistor becomes almost equal to zero, and the transistor is in the bottomed condition.

If the emitter is now made even more negative, the transistor remains bottomed and the output voltage continues to increase as the emitter, the base and the collector all move negatively together. When the input voltage V_1 is zero, the output voltage is almost equal to the supply voltage V_s. Now in this arrangement, the collector to base voltage of the transistor has never exceeded $V_s/2$ and the required swing of the input voltage V_1 is also equal to $V_s/2$, yet the output voltage can swing over the full range of the supply voltage V_s. Note that there is no current gain or phase inversion.

The writer has considered the theory of this form of amplifier in more detail elsewhere.[3] Suffice it to point out here that a very linear

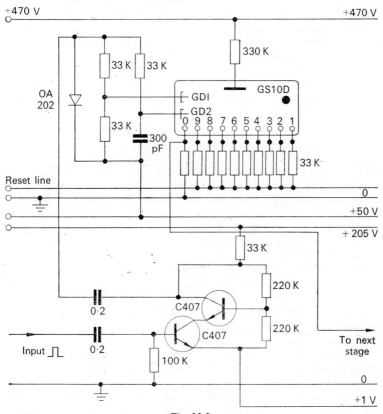

Fig. 13.5

voltage gain equal to two can be obtained. When driven from another transistor, the circuit takes the form of Figure 13.4. Here, the linearity of the output-input characteristic is increased by negative feedback from the output to the base of the second transistor via the resistive chain. This arrangement has been used by the writer very successfully for coupling dekatron selectors, the circuit arrangement being as shown in Figure 13.5.

13.7 DEKATRON COUPLING WITH VOLTAGE-DOUBLER

The circuit diagram of one stage of the form of dekatron selector used in early work on the present machines is shown in Figure 13.5. The use of such decimal counters in the prime number form of associating machine necessitates the arrangement of each counter to count a different prime number and then to re-start its count. After the required prime number is counted, the counter must give an output pulse and also be reset to zero ready to re-start its count.

This requires the use of additional circuitry, but it is not difficult to accomplish. However, the chief disadvantage of the dekatron form of counter in the present application is its large size, since the visual indication feature which is so valuable in other applications is not required at all here. An additional disadvantage is that the constructional labour requirement is excessive, since large numbers of counters are required in the prime number scheme.

13.8 TRANSISTOR-DIODE INTEGRATED CIRCUITS

At the present time there are many different forms of integrated switching circuit which might be used in the construction of the types of device considered here. The integrated circuits which have been used in the present work are from a low-cost diode-transistor logic range which uses a negative supply rail in addition to the normal positive supply rail. It is perhaps worth mentioning at this stage the reasons for the selection of these devices.

The design and use of such circuits has received intensive investigation in the past with discrete component circuits.[7, 9] The use of the diode-transistor form in industrial applications has shown its excellence for general-purpose use. It should perhaps be emphasised that in such general-purpose applications, unlike computer applications, the environment in which the devices must perform is relatively uncontrolled. This has introduced problems when attempts have been made to use integrated circuits, designed for computer use, in an industrial environment.

The use of diodes at the input to a unit can greatly reduce the problems encountered when units are interconnected. With some earlier forms of circuit, for example the resistor-transistor form, the performance obtained is very dependent on the output loading. With some other forms the available voltage swings are very small.

An important reason for the choice of the range selected is that in this range a negative bias supply rail is retained. Much attention has been devoted recently to the elimination of such rails in integrated circuits. It is perhaps useful to do so in digital computers, but for general purpose use the following points favour the retention of the negative bias supply rail:

(1) Improved noise immunity
(2) Reduced temperature effects
(3) Better pulse tolerance

All of these points are a consequence of the fact that elimination of a bias supply rail makes it difficult or impossible ever to cut off a transistor properly by reverse-biasing the base. If any current is flowing in the forward direction into the base terminal of a transistor, then the device retains a current gain from base to collector. Consequently, slight variations of the base current caused by noise, temperature variations or by signal variations are greatly amplified in the collector circuit of the transistor. This is no longer true if the base terminal is truly reverse-biased so that reverse base current flows. The transistor then behaves merely as two reverse-biased diodes and there is no amplification of the minor effects, as long as the transistor is cut-off.

The bias supply rail which is required does not have to supply a heavy current or to have a very closely controlled value of voltage. Thus it is not an expensive feature to provide. Consequently, the diode-transistor circuit using a negative bias supply rail as well as positive supply is well suited for the present application.

It should perhaps be mentioned that the range of integrated circuits adopted for the present work is no longer commercially available. Since it was the only known range which makes use of a negative bias supply rail, the devices will now be described briefly.

The circuit diagram of a typical unit of the type adopted, the OMY 120 *NOR* circuit, is shown in Figure 13.6.

The OMY range of integrated circuits was selected for use in the present research for the reasons outlined in the previous paragraph. The range uses a main supply voltage of $+6$ volts and a bias supply voltage of -6 volts. Diode-transistor logic is used. Physically, the T05 can size is used, fitted with ten leads. The various types of circuit used will now be described briefly.

The OMY120 is a three-input *NOR/NAND* gate using an *NPN* transistor. In the writer's terminology it is therefore a *PIN* circuit.[10] Three input diodes are fitted, and their common connection is brought out so that additional external diodes can be fitted. It is a notable

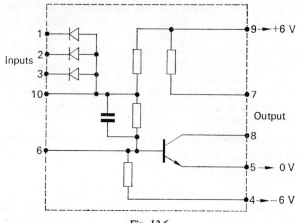

Fig. 13.6

feature of this circuit that every component interconnection is brought out to one of the terminations. Consequently in the event of an open-circuit failure of a component, caused for example by accidentally exceeding ratings during experimental work, an external component can easily be wired in its place.

The circuit is capable of supplying an output current of 13·5 mA. The output impedance with a positive output is 2900 ohms. This high value is immaterial with diode-transistor circuits, provided that the diodes at the inputs to the following stages have a high value of reverse resistance. An input current of 2·75 mA must be allowed for, so for absolute safety each circuit output should not feed more than four inputs (this is sometimes stated as 'fan-out = 4'). However, at room temperature it is safe to feed five inputs.

The input-voltage/output-voltage curves of this circuit come somewhere within a range which can be specified by two limiting curves. The usefulness of such circuits is determined by their ability to supply from their output terminals the inputs to other circuits. If two of these *PIN* circuits are connected together, with the output of each connected to the input of the other, a bistable circuit is formed. The output-input curves of the second circuit can be plotted on top of those for the first circuit as shown in Figure 13.7 since

$$V_{o1} = V_{i2} \quad \text{and} \quad V_{o2} = V_{i1}$$

The extent of the bistability is determined by the overlap areas of the curves, and thus these overlap areas can be taken as a measure of the compatibility of the circuits.

With these circuits, interfering noise pulses of about 0·5 volts

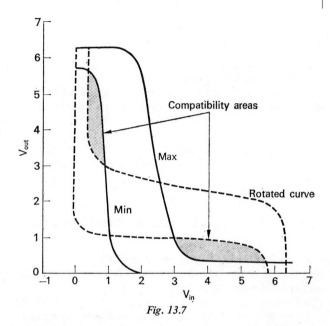

Fig. 13.7

amplitude will not cause malfunction. This is a valuable feature for use in experimental apparatus. On and off switching times of less than 0·1 microseconds are obtainable.

The OMY bistable integrated circuit has been used extensively in the present research, often in conjunction with the OMY122 steering circuit. Like the OMY120 gate, the OMY121 bistable circuit has the valuable experimental feature that every interconnection is brought out to an external terminal lead. This feature is unfortunately not shared by the OMY122 steering circuit. The OMY121 circuit is sometimes known as an R-S or Reset-Set flip-flop. It is capable of a counting speed of 2 MHz, which is ample. The compatibility and noise immunity figures are similar to those for the OMY120 gate described above.

The OMY121 bistable circuit can be converted into a monostable circuit if one of the feedback paths is immobilised by connecting terminal 2 to the zero line. The delay time is then determined by the time constant of an added external CR coupling circuit. The circuit can be triggered by positive pulses to pin 3 or via an external coupling circuit by negative pulses to pin 6. This arrangement has proved to be very useful in the present research.

External components can also be added to the basic bistable circuit to convert it to an astable circuit or to an emitter-coupled voltage-sensitive trigger.

13.9 BINARY-DECIMAL COUNTING METHODS

The feedback binary-decimal method of counting previously described by the writer was designed to overcome the spurious narrow 'spike' waveforms usually encountered in such arrangements.[2] These spikes occur when a stage which has just changed state is immediately changed back to its former state. In the method previously described, the spurious waveform was avoided by ensuring that a stage had always been settled down for a complete inter-pulse period before it was required to change state. Thus the state of the counter around the tens transfer point was:

9   0000
0   0001
0   0111   (middle digits changed by feedback from outer two)
1   1000

This arrangement has the following advantages:

(1) The middle digits have been steady for a complete inter-pulse period before they are changed by feedback.

(2) The feedback pulse, which is also used for tens transfer, starts at a time when only the least significant digit is changing.

(3) The feedback pulse is obtained on a definite output pulse rather than only while the output is changing.

(4) The tens transfer pulse is also used for feedback, so that no special outputs are required.

(5) At the time when the middle pulses are changing, they are not necessarily supplying output information since the first and last digits on their own give sufficient information.

These features make the method particularly attractive, and it appeared desirable to extend the system for use in the present prime-number counters. However, some thought about the system shows that it is unfortunately only suitable for use with even-number bases. The reason for this is that the transfer must always take place on the maintained occurrence of a particular value of the least significant digit. Consequently this method cannot be used for the present purpose, since the counters are required always to have an odd prime base. Many possibilities were considered. For example, one possibility is the use of counters always to count twice the required prime number, with a corresponding doubling of the input pulse repetition frequency. Another possibility is the acceptance of the 'spike' waveforms encountered in many other counting systems.

If binary counters incorporating transistors are to be used, there is little sense in incorporating double decoding, first from binary to decimal and then to a prime number. Such a course would only have advantages if a visual indication of the count was required, since to most people a decimal form is easier for rapid understanding.

In the present case a visual indication is desirable for setting-up purposes, so it is useful to have visually-indicating decimal test counters in the equipment. However, it is not necessary for all of the counters in the prime-period pulse system to have visual indication, and universal incorporation of this feature would add unnecessarily to the complexity and expense of the system. Details of the commercial binary-decimal counters with visual indication which were used in this work are not given here, since the counters were later retained only for test purposes.

13.10 POSSIBILITY OF COUNTING TWICE THE PRIME

One possible binary counting arrangement which was considered involved the detection of the condition when both the initial and the final digits first simultaneously achieved the value 1. This condition can then be used to change some of the central digits from 0 to 1 in such a way that the count ends with all stages of the counter set to 1 after a total number of input pulses equal to 2N–1, where N is the

Table 13.1. TWICE-PRIME COUNTING. The first time that the initial and final digits coincide with value 1, then some of the internal zeros are changed to ones as shown. The actual digits changed determine the prime number

1	00001		20	10100 → 11010	
2	00010		21	10101 → 11011	
3	00011		22	10110 → 11100	
4	00100		23	10111 → 11101	
5	00101		24	11000 → 11110	
6	0 0110		25	11001 → 11111	
7	00111		26	11010 → 00000	2×13
8	01000		27	011011	
9	01001		28	011100	
10	01010		29	011101	
11	01011		30	011110	
12	01100		31	011111	
13	01101		32	100000	
14	01110				
15	01111		33	100001 → 111111	
16	10000		34	100010 → 000000	2×17
17	10001 → 10111		33	100001 → 111011	
18	10010 → 11000		34	100010 → 111100	
19	10011 → 11001		35	100011 → 111101	
			36	100100 → 111110	
			37	100101 → 111111	
			38	100110 → 000000	2×19

required prime number. All stages of the counter will then attain the state zero simultaneously after a total number of input pulses equal to twice the required prime number N. The last few counts are then made equal to the complements of the first few, as required. The writer has discussed complementing binary codes elsewhere.[11] The method can best be illustrated by examples as shown in Table 13.1.

This method has two disadvantages. First, an additional multiway AND gate is required with each counter to obtain the 'all-zero's' output for recording.

It is not sufficient merely to record when the first and last digits are simultaneously zero. Secondly, it is required to produce a pulse only at the point where the first and last digits are equal to one for the first time. The necessity to ignore later coincidences involves circuit complexity.

13.11 PRIME NUMBER COUNTERS USING INTEGRATED CIRCUITS

For the present application, the counters are required to be adaptable for repetitive counting of any odd-prime base. A possible method is based on the earlier approach,[2] but the new method includes the use of a pulse delay of about one-half of the minimum interval between the master pulses which are to be counted. Such a delay is easily provided using an integrated monostable circuit, its use ensures the avoidance of 'spike' waveforms which tend to produce unreliability in counters.

To illustrate the method, consider a four-stage integrated-circuit binary counter as shown in Figure 13.8 with feedback arrangements added to cause the count to repeat after 13 input pulses rather than after 16 input pulses. Each bistable circuit is associated with a steering circuit. The circuit arrangement of the individual stages is identical to that of the discrete component decimal counter mentioned.

In order to count 13, the feedback is required to perform the following binary switching process:

10	1010	
11	1011	
12	1100	
12	1111	(after delay)
13 (0)	0000	
(1)	0001	and so on.

Thus, shortly after the counter indicates 1100 (i.e. 12), the state of the two least significant stages must be changed so that the counter indicates 1111. The next input pulse (the 13th) will then reset the counter to 0000. The digit state is changed by a NOR circuit which resets the required bistable stages to the 'one' state via diodes. In the

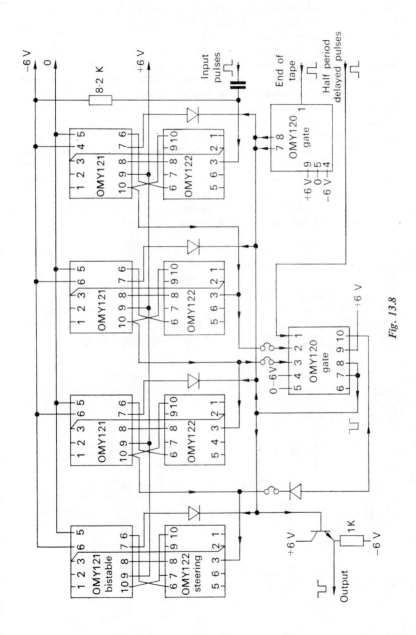

Fig. 13.8

case of the 13's counter, the resetting is accomplished whenever both of the most significant digits have the value one for the first time, i.e. whenever the count is 12.

The master resetting pulse is taken to the NOR resetting circuit via a delay monostable multivibrator, (also using integrated circuits). In this way, resetting does not occur until all stages have settled down: the narrow 'spike' waveforms previously mentioned are replaced by much longer pulses of about one-half of the standard length.

The length of the counting sequence, before resetting occurs, is determined by the inputs to the NOR resetting circuit. In practice all inputs to the NOR circuit, except the half-period delayed pulse, are taken to small sockets on the front of the counter unit, as are the outputs of the individual counter stages. In this way, the counting base is simply determined by the connections between the two sets of sockets. A standardised counter arrangement which can be set to count any required number base is thus achieved.

13.12 HALF-PERIOD PULSE DELAY

The system described requires the use of a central circuit supplying pulses delayed by one-half period after the main pulse input to the counters. These delayed pulses are provided by an integrated monostable delay circuit, using the arrangement of Figure 13.9.

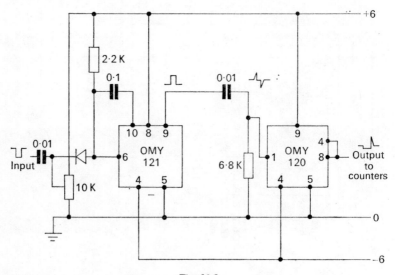

Fig. 13.9

Negative input pulses from the master-track playback amplifier are used to trigger the monostable circuit, which then gives a positive pulse of length equal to about one-half of the master-track pulse repetition period. Each pulse is differentiated, and the trailing-edge pulse is amplified and phase-inverted before being applied to the reset circuits of all counters.

REFERENCES

1. YOUNG, J. F., 'A Transistor Characteristic Curve Tracer', *Electronic Engineering*, **31**, 330 (1959)
2. YOUNG, J. F., 'Counters and Shift Registers Using Static Switching Units', *Electronic Engineering*, **37**, 161 (1965)
3. YOUNG, J. F., 'Coupling Dekatron Selectors with High-Voltage Transistors', *Electronic Engineering*, **39**, 323 (1967)
4. WARMAN, J. B., and BIBB, D. M., 'Transistor Circuits for use with Cold-Cathode Gas-Filled Multi-Cathode Counter Valves', *Electronic Engineering*, **30**, 136 (1958)
5. JOHANSON, E. W., 'Glow-Tube Programmer Controls Neutron Spectrometer Experiments', *Electronics*, **34**, 65, May (1961)
6. FRASER, H. J., 'Transistorized Dekatron Driving Circuits', *Electronic Engineering*, **34**, 40 (1962)
7. GRINICH, V. H., 'An Eighty-Volt Output Transistor Video Amplifier', *Trans. IRE*, **CT3**, 61 (1956)
8. SALAMAN, R. G., 'Receiver Video Transistor Amplifiers', *Trans. IRE*, **BTR4**, 68 (1958)
9. YOUNG, J. F., 'Transistor-Diode Static Switching Units', *Electronic Engineering*, **34**, 595, Sep. (1962)
10. YOUNG, J. F., 'Variable-Polarity Logic', *Control*, **9**, 493 Sep. (1965)
11. YOUNG, J. F., 'Cyclic Binary-Decimal Complementing Codes', *Control*, **8**, 226 May (1964)

14 | Conclusions

14.1 FALL-OUT FROM THIS FORM OF RESEARCH

Research such as that which has been carried out on the ASTRA associating machines leads to much industrial fall-out, rather as does the programme of space research. The reason for this is that the research is carried out by engineers, who are interested not only in the theoretical background to the work, but also to the practical use of its by-products. It is an unfortunate fact that a great deal of the research in cybernetics which has been supported very lavishly, particularly in the United States, has led to no practical results at all, though whole volumes of little-verified theory have appeared.

Even a modest programme of research such as the ASTRA programme produces results of direct application in practice if it is carried out in accordance with sound engineering practical principles. As an example, methods used on the ASTRA machines have been directly applied to traffic light controls using completely static equipment by Hollingshead of Aston. Protective gear using Hall effect devices appeared as a direct result of early ASTRA work. The symmetrical form of rectifier, and the triangular form of pulse-width modulation generator were developed because of need on the early machines. The use of square waves in the simplification of erase oscillators for tape recorders resulted from part of the research. There are many other examples which have appeared as a result of the other work in the laboratory.

14.2 PSEUDO-RANDOM BINARY COUNTERS

For use in the testing of cybernetic learning machines, some form of random testing device is required. It is not difficult to generate truly random signals using electrical noise. This is for example done on what is perhaps the best-known equipment of this type, the Electronic Random Number Indicating Equipment, commonly known as ERNIE.

The disadvantage of truly random pulse signals for test equipment is that a test must be carried out for a long time to ensure that the result really is dependent on a random input. The longer the time of the test the more nearly a true random result is likely. There are various ways of deciding on the statistical validity.

For testing electronic equipment however, it is desirable that a truly repeatable form of test should be available. This can be provided by a pseudo-random binary sequence generator. A binary shift register is provided with feedback from various stages to the input where the feedbacks are added together in a modulo-two form of adding circuit.

This form of pseudo-random generator was investigated by Bench at Aston and a special unit using integrated circuits for direct use with the ASTRA machines has been produced by Dixey.

Another reason for the development of practical forms of quasi-random generator at Aston has been the possibility of their use in the introduction of the feature of probability into the pulse-type associating machine. To achieve this, a random variation of pulse delay is required, and this is achieved by preventing the passage of a pulse until the next output pulse appears from a quasi-random generator.

14.3 SCAN FOR COMPUTER SIMULATION OF ASTRA PRINCIPLE

The principle of the ASTRA system has been simulated by Fisher at Aston. Fisher used his scanning retina device in order to provide the input to a PDP 9 computer, which was programmed to simulate various aspects of the ASTRA machines.

The 49 photo-cells of the retina to be scanned are switched to a trigger circuit by a uniselector. The trigger circuit then provides the input to the computer in serial form. The scanning uniselector is under the control of the computer. For this purpose a special computer program SAMPLE was written by Willets in MACRO machine language in the form of a FORTRAN function.

This function has the effect of halting the master computer program the first time that it is called, in order to allow:

(1) The scanning retina to be reset to the start position if necessary.
(2) The analogue to digital convertor on the computer to be set to the input channel connected.
(3) The word length to be set to 6 bits.

The sampling is accomplished by the following procedure. The relay bank is called up and the relay contacts are instructed to close. The computer is then instructed to perform a delaying calculation which takes 3 microseconds. A constant S in the program determines how many times this delay shall be repeated in order to obtain a total delay of 37 milliseconds. This delay provides sufficient time for the relay contacts in the computer to be closed, for the relay in the artificial retina unit to operate, and for the ratchet of the uniselector to set.

An instruction is then passed to the computer relay circuit for the relay to be opened, and there is then a further delay of 22 milliseconds as determined by a further constant T set in this program. This allows sufficient time for the wiper of the uniselector to be advanced to the next contact. An instruction is then given to the analogue digital convertor to sample the output voltage and to note whether the voltage is positive or negative.

The above procedure is repeated 49 times, that is once for each of the 49 photo-cells in the scanning retina which is to provide the input to the computer. The results of the scan are stored in the computer, and then the uniselector is reset by taking it one further step. The complete retina scanning procedure takes about 3 seconds.

14.4 DIRECT INDUSTRIAL USE OF ASTRA

The ASTRA form of associating machine has direct application to the control of machine tools and to the control of conveyor systems in industry. This fall-out from the research was certainly not expected or planned for, since the object was to design and build extendable machines which could be used for further extension and investigation into learning and intelligent activity by machines.

The basic ASTRA MK. 3 machine has 100 nerve inputs and 10 muscle outputs. Now if each of these outputs is used to control a different movement or operation on a machine tool, then the machine tool can be operated by a human simply by pressing the correct one, or more, from the ten output buttons.

Now suppose that the human operator presses the buttons in such a way as to cause the machine tool to make a certain component. If, while the human is carrying out the task, one of the nerve inputs is stimulated, the complete sequence of operations will be recorded in the machine memory, associated with that particular nerve input.

If then in future that particular nerve input is stimulated, the machine will produce the correct sequence of outputs to the machine tool to cause it to make the corresponding component, provided that it has material upon which to work. In this way, the ASTRA machine can be taught to control the machine tool to make any of 100 different components in response to the stimulation of a particular one of the 100 nerve inputs. A complete day's production programme can be supplied to the machine on punched or magnetic tape.

14.5 FINAL CONCLUSION

The work described in this book has led to the simulation of some aspects of the operation of the animal nervous system which meets the basic requirements laid down by MacKay.[1] These requirements are for '...a statistical model in which connections between elements (1) are incompletely specified, (2) function with adjustable probability, and (3) grow in complexity step by step with the development of internal organisation to match the structure of the environment'.

It is an unfortunate fact that MacKay's statement appears in one of the lesser-known publications. Indeed, the writer only came across it very recently, even though it expresses in a concise form the basis of much of the programme of investigation which has been carried out on the ASTRA machines.

Although the methods being used at the present time are those using pulse recirculation, it is quite possible that there will be a return later to some of the earlier methods if these prove to have some engineering, economic or reliability advantages.

14.6 THE FUTURE AND CYBERNETIC ENGINEERING

The robot age is with us now. The present problem is simply one of economics. Those countries which are prepared to spend money now on the development of the low-cost domestic and industrial robot will reap their rewards in the near future. The earliest low cost robots to be developed will have tremendous economic advantages over later devices. Only the economics of scale can hold the price of the robot down to the point where large-scale sales will result. Only large-scale sales will hold down the price.

Thus it is urgent that those countries which wish to take advantage of the initial world-wide impact of the low-cost robot should invest now. And it is becoming apparent that this fact is being realised in some countries. The robot revolution, when it comes, will be quite unlike any earlier form of industrial revolution. The robots produced will themselves be capable of reproducing their kind since they will be capable of operating the industrial machinery upon which they have been produced.

For man, the implications of the present state of knowledge is clear. His leisure time will increase drastically in the next few years. How man will react to this fact remains to be seen, but he will adapt to the new conditions, even as he has adapted to the conditions of life imposed by the existence of the hydrogen bomb.

Or am I being over-optimistic?

REFERENCES

1. MACKAY, D. M., 'Modelling of Large-Scale Nervous Activity', *S.E.B. Symposium*, No. 14, 192 (1960)

Index